T: 10   S: $\frac{1}{7}$
H: 9
$\frac{46}{7}$·50 (I think
       it is HC
       w/ no DJ

A Programmed Introduction to

THE GAME OF CHESS

M. W. Sullivan

Fred Reinfeld comments

A famous writer once made the observation that the reader of a book goes through the same process as the author did — but in reverse order. It follows that where the author has worked hard to express himself clearly and logically, the reader will have a comparatively easy job of following in the author's footsteps.

This ideal state of affairs ought to apply to chess, but unfortunately it doesn't, as a rule. When we examine most chess primers we get the impression that the author was blithely unaware of the difficulties that a beginner is likely to experience.

Precisely this aspect, which is generally overlooked by most chess writers, is the one on which Dr. Sullivan has concentrated most heavily in his admirable exposition of the game. He has taken the utmost care to guide the reader step by step, presenting each phase with marvelous patience and gentle insistence. The order of the subject matter has been planned with the greatest care, so that the reader is cleverly led from the simplest details to more advanced material. Unobtrusive review questions keep the reader on the alert without boring him or burdening him.

All this, to my way of thinking, amounts to great teaching such as few in our time are capable of. It requires enormous ability — and almost super-human patience — to construct a course of study so lovingly worked out to the tiniest detail; and it takes the most devoted of teachers to work so tirelessly, so painstakingly, and so rewardingly in the reader's interest.

In the past, I have often been painfully surprised to see that people who had read what seemed to be excellent introductions to the game nevertheless had astonishing misconceptions about some of the elementary details. This is something that will never happen to anyone who studies Dr. Sullivan's masterly introduction to the game. The beauty of this book, to my way of thinking, is that it serves as an admirable introduction to the game, no matter what your future intentions about chess may be. If you want to regard the game as a delightful hobby and form of relaxation, you will find your knowledge of the game quite adequate. If you want to continue and deepen your study of chess — and I sincerely hope you do — you will find that Dr. Sullivan's admirable work forms the perfect base for more advanced study.

Whether or not the reader is aware of the startlingly original nature of this book, he will benefit enormously from his study of it. Nevertheless, as a simple act of justice to Dr. Sullivan, I think it only fair to state my opinion that this is the most revolutionary book ever written on chess — a work that is destined to have a profound influence on all worthwhile chess books of the future. Dr. Sullivan has left us all — writers as well as readers — in his debt.

FRED REINFELD

Fred Reinfeld is a chess master and the author of over fifty chess books.

About the author

In addition to his doctorate, M. W. Sullivan has two master's degrees and two bachelor's degrees. He has taught at the Choate School, the University of Puerto Rico, Yale University, Marquette University, and was formerly head of the modern language department and director of graduate studies in modern languages at Hollins College.

Dr. Sullivan was one of the principal investigators for a Carnegie Foundation grant in automated teaching media. He has also directed two institutes under the National Defense Education Act.

The author of three books, five programmed courses and numerous other publications, Dr. Sullivan is now president of a research organization devoted to the preparation of programmed materials for school use.

About the program

The original version of this course was tested on a large group of subjects which included some of the nation's finest programmers. Their errors, comments, and suggestions for changes were recorded and compiled. Frame by frame, the course was rewritten and expanded to include additional material. This whole process was then repeated five more times. Over one hundred people helped write this course. This means that, unlike most books, it is not one man's approach to teaching the subject but an actual record of the way that many people have learned to play chess.

Thus programmed learning offers a number of advantages to an author. He can repeatedly test every sentence of his text with large groups of people. Their errors and comments can be compiled frame by frame. The author doesn't release his program until his readers' satisfaction is very high and their error rate is very low.

The advantages of programmed learning for the reader are even greater than those for the writer. You will go through this book at your own speed. As you learn each new step, you will be asked questions about it, and you will check your answers immediately. Thus you will always be sure that you are really mastering the material.

Introduction

Chess is our oldest and most popular intellectual pastime. It is a game for two players which uses a board and special pieces. The players sit on opposite sides of the board. They are designated White and Black. This is all you need to know in order to begin the study of "The Royal Game."

You will find that the left-hand pages of *The Game of Chess* are upside-down and backwards. Pay no attention to them until you have finished all of the right-hand pages.

You may give your answers orally, write them in this book, or write them on a separate sheet of scrap paper. After you have given each answer, check it by pulling down your slider.

Answers separated by a comma may be given in either order. Answers placed one above the other must be given in the listed order.

Here are some sample "frames" designed to help you use *The Game of Chess.* Cover the answers on the right with your slider.

Black decides to move

9. K-K1

This is a mistake. He could have prolonged the game by moving ...K-K3, but checkmate would have been inevitable in five moves, starting with 10. Q-KN4 ch.

After 9. ...K-K1, White has a checkmate in two moves beginning with

10. Q-KR5 ch

Black's only possible reply is

10. _____   ...P-KN3

∞

What move will checkmate Black?

11. _____   QxP mate

∞

Note that Black had not moved a single piece from the first rank. Don't make his mistake. Develop your _____ and Bishops as rapidly as possible.   Knights

—477—

You have now learned all that you need to know in order to enjoy playing Chess. Play against the strongest opponents available. You will find that you learn from each game, and that your own play improves rapidly as you put into practice the moves and techniques you have studied in this program.

∞

Remember to be a courteous opponent. Never take back a move. Once you have taken your hand off a piece, you cannot change the move. If you touch a piece, you must move it if it is legally possible. If you touch one of your opponent's pieces, you must capture it if it is possible for you to do so.

∞

Now, play Chess! I hope that you will enjoy it as much as I have.

M. W. SULLIVAN

—00—

The title of this book is THE _____ OF CHESS.   GAME

(Give your answer; then pull your
slider down and check.)

—01—

This —is/isn't— a programmed introduction to the game of   is
chess.

(Choose the correct word.)

—02—

You will prefer to write some of your answers. May other
answers be given orally?   yes

—03—

Questions which can be answered by "yes" or "no" are not
followed by blanks because such answers are always —oral/   oral
written.

—04—

When you reach a blank, like the one at the end of this
sentence, you will give an oral or written _____.   answer

—05—

May answers be written in the blanks in this book?   yes

—06—

May they be written on a piece of scrap paper?   yes

	White		Black
2.	P-Q4	2.	PxP

Note that White is potentially two steps ahead in his development. He has moved both his King Pawn and his Queen Pawn to open up diagonals for both his _____. Black has moved neither of these Pawns.

Bishops

_____

∞

3.	N-KB3	3.	P-K4
4.	P-QB3		

**Position after
6. ...P-KR3?**

White exchanges a Pawn to get rid of Black's Pawn on Q5, so that he can develop his Knight to QB3.

		4.	PxP
5.	NxQBP	5.	P-Q3
6.	B-QB4	6.	P-KR3?

Check with the diagram.

∞

White has developed both Knights and a Bishop; Black has made nothing but Pawn moves. White's superiority in development makes possible an immediate attack on the Black King. He first sacrifices a Bishop by moving

7. _____ ch

BxKBP ch

_____

∞

Black then plays

7. _____

...KxB

_____

∞

8. NxP ch

If Black plays ...PxN, White will play _____.

QxQ

_____

∞

Black therefore plays

8. K-K2

How can White continue the attack with his Queen Knight? 9. _____

N-Q5 ch

—07—

Questions which are not followed by blanks are to be answered *—orally/in writing.*

| | orally |

—08—

After you give each answer, should you pull your slider down and check?

| | yes |

—09—

If you see two answers which look like this

King, Knight

the comma between them means that they *—must be given in that order/may be given in either order.*

| | may be given in either order |

—010—

Must two answers which look like this

King
Knight

be given in the listed order?

| | yes |

—011—

Before looking at the next page, you will cover the answer column with your _____.

| | slider |

—012—

Always give your answer *—before/after—* you pull the slider down to check.

| | before |

—013—

Now turn to page 1, cover the answers with your slider, and begin studying THE GAME OF _____.

| | CHESS |

—475—

What move will checkmate
Black? _____

R(QB7)-KN7 mate

—476—

Set up the pieces in their starting positions, with the White
chessmen on your side of the board. In playing the opening,
remember to get your Knights and then your Bishops out onto
the board as fast as possible. Don't waste time by moving the
same piece several times and, above all, don't make useless
Pawn moves. It will usually be necessary to move only two
Pawns to get your other pieces out onto the board. These are
the _____ Pawn and the _____ Pawn.

King, Queen

∞

The game which follows is an example of what can happen if
one player wastes his time with useless Pawn moves, while
his opponent is developing his Knights and Bishops:

White	Black
1. P-K4	1. P-QB4

When Black answers 1. P-K4 with 1. ...P-QB4, the opening
is called a Sicilian _____.

Defense

∞

— 1 —

Like Checkers, Chess is played by _____ players.

2

— 2 —

The game of Chess is played on a board which is the same as a checkerboard. When used for Chess, this board is called a _____.

chessboard

— 3 —

This is a picture of a CHESSBOARD.

It measures ____ squares in either direction and has a total of _____ squares.

8
64

— 4 —

Take out your chessboard and place it in front of you as it is in the picture.

You should have a light square in the —right/left— hand corner nearest to you.

right

—473—

What is White's best move? _____

∞

Why not P-KN8/Q?

∞

Why not P-KN8/N ch?

P-KN8/R

Black would be
stalemated.

Since the remaining
White Pawn would
queen in this case, this
would also lead to a
win, but much more
slowly since the Rook
is stronger than the
Knight.

—474—

White has doubled his Rooks on
the Queen file. He can checkmate
Black in two moves. His first move
is _____.

∞

What is Black's only possible move? ..._____

∞

White then plays _____.

R-Q8 ch

...RxR

RxR mate

— 5 —

The game of Checkers is played on only the dark squares. Unlike Checkers, Chess is played on both the _____ and the _____ squares.

light, dark

— 6 —

In Chess, the light squares are called the WHITE SQUARES. The dark squares are called the _____ squares.

black

— 7 —

The two players move alternately. In other words, a player —can/cannot— make two consecutive moves. He moves, waits for his opponent to move, and then moves again.

cannot

— 8 —

The pieces that you use to play Chess are called CHESSMEN.

How many white chessmen are there? _____

16

∞

Are there sixteen black chessmen?

yes

∞

This makes a total of _____ chessmen.

32

—471—

White can force a checkmate in two moves.

His first move is _____.

N-KB6 ch

∞

Black's only possible move is ..._____.

...K-KR1

∞

White then moves _____.

R-KN8 mate

—472—

Sometimes a Chess player will under-promote a Pawn. That is to say, he will replace it with a Rook, Knight, or Bishop instead of a Queen when it reaches the eighth rank. He usually does this either to checkmate his opponent immediately, or to avoid stalemating him.

What two moves will checkmate Black? _____,
_____

P-QN8/N mate,
B-K2 mate

∞

Would White win if he promoted the Pawn to a Queen, Rook or Bishop?

no

∞

Why not?

Black would be stalemated.

—9—

The smallest chessmen are called PAWNS.
A Pawn has a ball on top.

Is this a picture of a Pawn?

∞

yes

There are _____ White and _____ Black
Pawns.

8, 8

—10—

The tallest chessman is called the KING.
The King has a crown with a cross on top.

This is a picture of a _____.

∞

King

How many White Kings are there? _____

∞

1

Does each side have only one King?

yes

—11—

You have now learned the names
of two chessmen. These are the
_____ and the _____.

King, Pawn

—12—

There are eight _____ and one _____ on
each side.

Pawns
King

White	Black
13. P-KB7 ch	

What is the only move which will save Black's Rook?

13. _____   ...KxP

∞

| 14. N-KN5 ch | 14. K-KN1 |
| 15. B-QB4 ch | |

Interposing the Queen or the Rook will now only prolong Black's agony. If he moves ...K-KR1, White plays _____ mate.   QxP

Black therefore moves

15.   K-KB1

∞

White can now checkmate Black with a Knight move. This move is

16. _____   NxP mate

—470—

The following diagrams will illustrate a series of checkmate situations.

If it is Black's move, the position is a _____ and the game is a _____.   stalemate
                                                                        draw

∞

If it is White's move, he wins by moving _____.   B-QN2 mate
(This is the last move of a forced checkmate with King, Knight, and Bishop.)

—13—

The second tallest piece is called the QUEEN. The Queen has a crown with notches in it.

This is a picture of a _____.

∞

How many Queens are there on each side? _____

Queen

1

—14—

The piece which looks like a horse's head is called a KNIGHT.

Is this a picture of a Knight?

∞

no

This is a picture of a _____.

∞

Pawn

This is a picture of a —*King/Knight*.

∞

Knight

How many White Knights are there? _____

2

∞

How many Black Knights are there? _____

2

	White		Black
		9.	B-QB4
10.	P-QB3	10.	O-O
11.	Q-K4		

What is White's threat? _____

∞

QxKRP mate

_____

11.   P-KB4

This seems to be a strong reply to White's threat. It simultaneously defends the Black Bishop on KN5 and attacks the White Queen. White's attack along the diagonal on Black's KRP seems to be permanently blocked. How can you eliminate the effects of this move with the power of the Pawn which you have just learned?

PxP e.p. (*en passant*)

12.   _____

_____

∞

Position after
12. PxP e.p.

Check with the diagram to make sure that you have done this correctly.

∞

12.   R-K1

This move pins the White _____.

Queen

∞

This means that White will have to continue his attack with a checking move. If he leaves Black free for a move, Black will play ..._____.

...RxQ ch

∞

—15—

The piece that looks like a miniature tower, or the turret on a castle, is called a ROOK.

Is this a picture of a Rook?   no

∞

This is a picture of a _____.   King

∞

This is a picture of a —Queen/Rook.   Rook

∞

How many Black Rooks are there? _____   2

∞

There are also _____ White Rooks.   2

—16—

The only Chess piece that we have not named is the BISHOP. On top it has a Bishop's mitre with a slit in it.

Is this a picture of a Bishop?   no

∞

This is a picture of a _____.   Knight

∞

This is a picture of a —Rook/Bishop.   Bishop

∞

There are _____ Black Bishops and_____ White Bishops.   2, 2

Position after
6. ...PxP e.p.

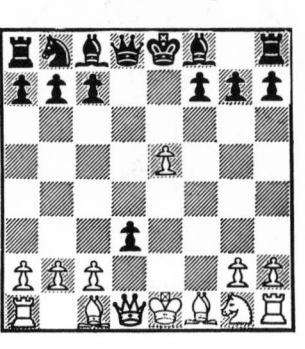

Black moves his Pawn from K5 to Q6, the square which the White Queen Pawn would be on if it had moved forward only one square instead of two. He removes White's Queen Pawn from the board exactly as he would any other captured piece. He has captured the Pawn *en passant* (abbreviated "*e.p.*").

Check with the diagram to see that you have made this move correctly. It is a move which you will seldom see, but, as this game demonstrates, you should be aware of its existence.

∞

White	Black
7. BxQP	7. N-QB3

This move attacks White's Pawn on K5.

How can White defend it with a Knight move?
    8. _____

N-KB3

∞

What move will pin White's Knight?
                    8. _____

...B-KN5

∞

Why does this move indirectly attack White's Pawn on K5?

Black threatens to play ...NxP.

∞

Why couldn't White then play NxN?

Black would play ...BxQ.

∞

The White Knight is _____ by the Black Bishop.

pinned

∞

    9. Q-K2

This move defends the White _____ _____.

King Pawn

∞

—17—

Here are pictures of all the chessmen. Circle the picture of a Pawn.

—18—

Circle the picture of a Rook.

—19—

Circle the picture of the King.

—468—

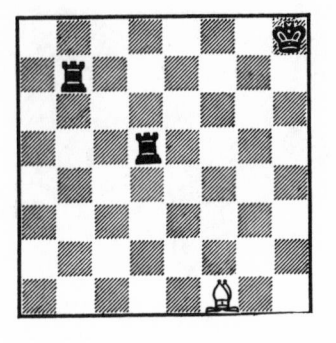

What is White's best move?_____

B-KN2
(pinning one Black Rook against the other. Black can move only one of the Rooks. White will then capture the other one.)

—469—

Set up the pieces in their starting positions, with the White chessmen on your side of the board. Make the following moves:

	White		Black
1.	P-K4	1.	P-K4
2.	N-QB3	2.	N-KB3
3.	P-KB4	3.	P-Q4
4.	BPxP	4.	NxP
5.	NxN	5.	PxN
6.	P-Q4		

Check with the diagram.

∞

Position after 6. P-Q4

Black now takes advantage of a very rarely used power of the Pawn. This is called capturing EN PASSANT.

When a player moves a Pawn forward two squares, his opponent has a right to capture it, as if it had moved only one square, providing that he does this on his next move and that he does it with a Pawn. Hence Black now has the right to capture the White Pawn on Q4, *en passant.*

—20—

Circle the picture of a Knight.

—21—

Circle the picture of the Queen.

—22—

Circle the picture of a Bishop.

—465—

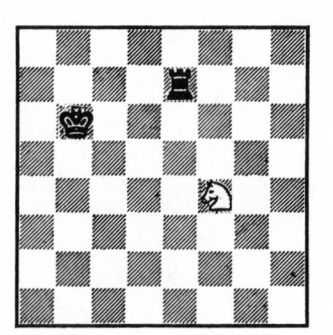

What is White's best move?_____

B-KR3
(winning the Queen
with a pin)

—466—

What is White's best move?_____

N-Q5 ch
(winning the Black
Rook with a fork)

—467—

What is White's best move?_____

R-Q5
(forking the Bishop
and the Knight)

Why not R-KB8, pinning the
Bishop?

Black saves the Bishop
by moving ...K-QB1,
or ...K-QB2.

—23—

This is a picture of a —*Rook/Knight*.

Rook

—24—

This is a picture of a _____.

Knight

—25—

Is this a picture of a Rook?

∞

This is a picture of the _____.

no

King

Can the Queen capture the Pawn?

∞

Why not?

∞

White	Black

11. QxB

Since White's Queen was lost in any event, he tries to get something in exchange.

Black will now move

11. _____

∞

In material, _____ is now a Bishop ahead.

∞

Nevertheless White resigns. Why?

─────────────────────

—464—

In the following diagrams we shall review some ways of winning material.

What is White's best move?_____

Right column answers:

no

─────────────────────

White's King would be in check. The Queen is pinned by the Bishop.

─────────────────────

...NxQ

─────────────────────

White

─────────────────────

There is no way to prevent Black from playing 12. ...PxR/Q

─────────────────────

R-KR6 ch
(winning the Queen with an x-ray attack)

—26—

This is a picture of the _____.

Queen

—27—

This is a picture of a —*Pawn/Bishop.*

Bishop

—28—

This is a picture of a _____.

Pawn

White	Black	
	6. N-KN3	

This move attacks not only the Pawn on K5 but also the White _____.

Bishop

_____

∞

| 7. B-KN3 | 7. Q-QR4! | |

Black prepares a discovered check.

8. Q-Q5

What is the only move which will place the White King in check?

8. _____

...P-QN6 dis ch

_____

∞

What is the only way that White can capture the Black Queen?

9. _____

QxQ

_____

∞

Black does not recapture the Queen. He relies on a Pawn promotion and a pin to gain an overwhelming advantage in material. What move will attack the Rook on White's QR1?

9. _____

...P-QN7

_____

∞

10. Q-QB3

This was the only possibility of recapturing the Black Pawn when it queened, but Black destroys even this hope with a powerful pin. He moves

10. _____

...B-QN5

∞

—29—

The light chessmen are always referred to as White.

We refer to the dark chessmen as _____ .

Black

___

—30—

You will now learn the positions which the White chessmen (or pieces) occupy at the beginning of a game. We shall refer to these positions as the STARTING POSITIONS for the White pieces.

Pick up your two White Rooks. Place them in the nearest right and left-hand corners of the board. Check with the diagram.

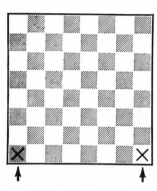

∞

Note that there is a _____ square in the right-hand corner nearest to you.

white

___

—31—

Pick up your two White Knights. Place them on the squares next to the Rooks. Check with the diagram.

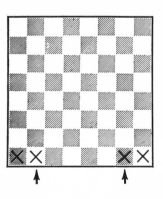

—463—

Set up the pieces in their starting positions, with the Black chessmen on your side of the board. Make the following moves:

White	Black
1. P-K4	1. P-QB4

This is called a SICILIAN DEFENSE.

    2. P-QN4

White offers a gambit Pawn with the hope of building up a strong center.

	2. PxP
3. P-Q4	3. P-K4

Black gives the Pawn back to accelerate his own development.

4. PxP	4. N-QB3

This move attacks White's Pawn on K5. How can White defend it with a Knight move?

    5. _____

                    ∞

          5. KN-K2

Where will this Knight eventually move to attack White's Pawn on K5? _____

                    ∞

    6. B-KB4

White hastens to defend the Pawn. Check with the diagram.

N-KB3

_____

KN3

_____

Position after
6. B-KB4

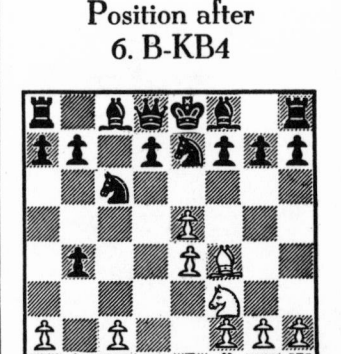

—32—

Pick up your two White Bishops and place them next to the Knights. Check with the diagram.

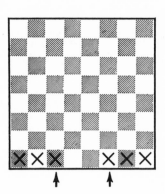

—33—

Pick up the White Queen. Place this piece on the remaining white square in the first row. The Queen is always set up on her "color." In the starting position, the White Queen is always on a _____ square.

white

—34—

Place the White King on the remaining black square in the first row. Check with the diagram.

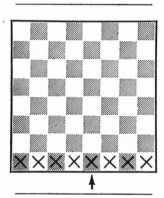

∞

Are these the starting positions of the White pieces in the first row?

yes

∞

Now take all the White pieces off the board.

White will then move _____ .

P-QR7

∞

_____

And Black will move ..._____ .

...K-QB3

∞

_____

White will then move _____ .

P-QR8/Q ch

∞

_____

Now the Black King ―*can*/*cannot*― capture the White Queen.

cannot

∞

_____

With the superiority of a Queen, White has ―*drawn*/*lost*/*won*― the game.

won

_____

_____

―462―

Place the White King on KB1, and a White Pawn on KB7; place the Black King on KR1.

If it is White's move, he wins the game with _____ .

P-KB8/Q ch

∞

_____

But if it is Black's move, he plays ..._____ .

...K-KN2

∞

_____

If White then plays P-KB8/Q ch, Black plays ..._____ , and the game is a _____ .

...KxQ
draw

—35—

You have just learned the starting positions which the White pieces occupy in the first row at the beginning of the game of Chess. Now let's review them.

First, place the White King and Queen in their starting positions. Then check with the picture.

(The Queen should be on a white square to the left of the King.)

∞

Now place the White Bishops in their starting positions and check with the picture.

∞

Place the White Knights in their starting positions and check.

∞

Place the White Rooks in their starting positions and check.

∞

Leave the White pieces in their starting positions in the first row.

Black will move ..._____.

∞

White will move _____.

∞

Black will move ..._____.

∞

White will move _____.

∞

Black will move ..._____, and the game is a _____.

∞

Leaving the White King on KR1, return the White Pawn to QR4, and the Black King to KB6. We saw that, when the pieces were in these positions and it was ―*Black's/White's*― move, the game was a draw.

∞

Now let's see what happens when it is White's move.

White will move _____.

∞

And Black will move ..._____.

∞

White will move _____.

∞

And Black will move ..._____.

∞

...K-QB3

P-QR7

...K-QN2

P-QR8/Q ch

...KxQ
draw

Black's

P-QR5

...K-K5

P-QR6

...K-Q4

The starting position of the White King is on the —*right / left*—
of the White Queen.

right

_____

—37—

The horizontal rows of squares on the chessboard are called
RANKS. The White pieces are on the first horizontal row;
we could also say that they are on the first _____.

rank

_____

—38—

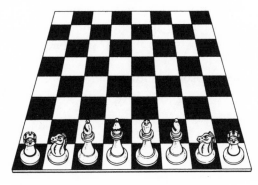

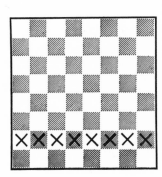

Place the eight White Pawns on the eight squares of the
second rank. Check with the diagram.

∞

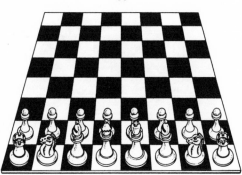

These are the _____ positions for all of the _____
chessmen.

starting
White

∞

Remove all chessmen from the board.

If it is White's move, he will either move _____ or _____ to protect the Pawn.

K-KB6, K-Q6

∞

Since it makes no difference, let us assume that he moves K-Q6. Black's only possible move is ..._____.

...K-KB2

∞

White will then move _____.

K-Q7

∞

And White will win the game, since Black must now move away and let the Pawn _____.

queen

∞

With the superiority of a _____, checkmate is now assured.

Queen

—461—

As you have just seen, in a King and Pawn ending, whether you win or draw may depend upon whose move it is.

Place a White Pawn on QR4, and the White King on KR1; place the Black King on KB6. If it is Black's move, he will play ..._____, in an effort to capture the Pawn.

...K-K5

∞

White will play _____.

P-QR5

∞

Black will then move ..._____.

...K-Q4

∞

White will move _____.

P-QR6

∞

—39—

Examine the symbols on this chessboard. Henceforth, we shall use these symbols instead of pictures of the pieces. Notice that the symbols for the Rooks, Knights, Bishops, and Pawns look very much like the chessmen themselves.

The Queen is symbolized by a spiked crown. The remaining piece, symbolized by a rounded crown with a cross on it, is the _____.

King

—40—

Set up all the White chessmen in their starting positions. Check with the diagram.

∞

Leave the White chessmen in their starting positions.

—41—

This is the symbol for a _____.

Rook

—458—

If a player who is not in check cannot move without placing his King in check, we know that he is _____.

stalemated

∞

If his King is in check, and he has no move which will get the King out of check, we know that he is _____.

checkmated

—459—

If it is Black's move,
he is _____.

stalemated

∞

If it is White's move, he has to choose between moving away and letting Black _____ the Pawn, or moving to _____, where he protects the Pawn, but stalemates the Black King.

capture
KR6

∞

In either case, the game is a _____.

draw

—460—

Place the Black King on K1; place a White Pawn on K7, and the White King on K6. If it is Black's move, the position is a _____, and the game is a _____.

stalemate
draw

∞

—42—

This is the symbol for a _____.

Knight

—43—

This is the symbol for a _____.

Queen

—44—

This is the symbol for a _____.

Bishop

—45—

This is the symbol for a _____.

Pawn

—46—

This is the symbol for a _____.

King

∞

You are already familiar with two types of forced draws; these are stalemate and _____ check.

| | perpetual |

—457—

Set up your chessmen in accordance with the diagram:

Black has an enormous material advantage of a Rook and a Pawn.

What are three moves which would checkmate White?

..._____ ,

..._____ ,

..._____

	Q-KR8 mate,
	...Q-KN8 mate,
	...R-K8 mate

∞

But it is White's move, so he has a last chance to parry Black's threats. White can force a draw by moving _____.

| | Q-KB7 ch |

∞

What is Black's only possible move? ..._____

| | ...K-KR1 |

∞

White will then move _____.

| | Q-KB8 ch |

∞

Black's only possible move is ..._____.

| | ...K-KR2 |

∞

And White will move _____.

| | Q-KB7 ch, etc. |

∞

The game is a draw by _____ _____.

| | perpetual check |

—47—

The White chessmen are in their starting positions. Now set up the Black pieces in accordance with the symbols in the diagram.

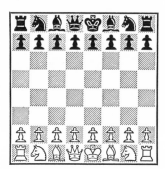

Notice that the Black Rooks, Knights, and Bishops are opposite the White Rooks, Knights, and Bishops. The Black Queen is opposite the White _____.

Queen

—48—

In the starting position, the Queen is always on her color. This means that the Black Queen is on a _____ square.

black

—49—

The Black King is opposite the _____ _____.

White King

—50—

The White Queen is on the white square to the left of the White _____.

King

∞

For the person playing Black, the Black Queen is on the black square to the _____ of the Black King.

right

White's first move in forcing the checkmate will be _____.

R-KR6 ch

∞

The Black King must move to the _____ rank.

second

∞

White will then move _____.

R-QR7 ch

∞

The Black King is forced to the _____ rank.

first

∞

White then moves _____.

R-KR8 mate

∞

If the Black King is able to move over diagonally to a point where he could capture a Rook on one of its checking moves, White simply moves the Rook over toward the other side of the board, and continues to force checkmate in the same way.

—456—

At any time during a Chess game, one of the players may resign if he feels that there is no chance for him to win or draw the game. The two players may also, at any time, agree to draw the game.

A game is also drawn if neither player has sufficient material left to checkmate the other. An example of this would be a game in which you have only a King and a _____ or Bishop left against your opponent's lone King.

Knight

∞

—51—

For the person playing White, the White King is on the right of the White _____.

∞

For the person playing Black, the Black King is on the _____ of the Black Queen.

∞

Now remove all the chessmen from the board.

—52—

Set up the White pieces in their starting positions on the first rank. This means that you will omit the _____ because they are on the _____ rank.

∞

Check with the diagram.

Queen

left

Pawns
second

Black will be forced to move to a square on the _____ file.

QB

∞

White will then move _____.

R-QB7 ch

∞

The Black King is forced to move to a square on the _____ file.

QN

∞

White's next move is _____.

Q-QN8 ch

∞

The Black King must move to the _____ file.

QR

∞

White then moves _____.

R-QR7 mate

∞

Is this checkmate with Queen and Rook just as easy with the Queen on one side of the board and the Rook on the other?

yes

—455—

Two Rooks can checkmate the Black King by forcing him back to the edge of the board just as the Queen and Rook did.

Place the Black King on K3; place one White Rook on QR5, and the other White Rook on KR3. The Black King cannot advance beyond the _____ rank.

third

∞

—53—

You have learned that the horizontal rows on the chessboard are called _____.

∞

The vertical rows are called FILES. These are pictures of a rank and a file. Circle the picture of a file.

ranks

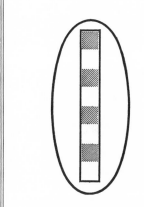

—54—

The files are named after the pieces that stand on them in their starting positions in the first rank. Circle the picture of a Rook file.

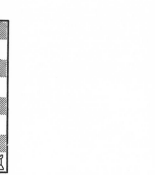

Rook

—55—

The files at the extreme left and the extreme right of the chessboard are called the _____ files.

In the present position, it is obvious that the Black King can never move past his fourth rank, because he would be moving into check from the White _____ .

Rook

∞

White's first move in forcing the checkmate is Q-KB5 ch. The King must move to some square in his third rank. It makes no difference which one. Let us say that Black moves K-QB3. White now moves R-KN6 ch. And now the King is forced to move to his _____ rank.

second

∞

Let us assume that he moves to QN2. What will probably be White's next move? _____

Q-KB7 ch (Q-Q7 ch is just as good.)

∞

Black is forced back to his _____ rank.

first

∞

Whatever square he moves to, White will checkmate him on the following move with _____ .

R-KN8 mate

—454—

Place the Black King on Q6; place a White Rook on K7, and the White Queen on KB8. The Black King cannot advance beyond his _____ file.

Queen

∞

White's first move in forcing checkmate will be _____ .

Q-Q8 ch

∞

—56—

The files next to the Rook files are called the _____ files.

Knight

—57—

The files to the inside of the board from the Knight files are called the _____ _____.

Bishop files

—58—

The two central files are called the (read from left to right for White) _____ and _____ files.

Queen
King

—59—

The starting positions of the White pieces are always shown at the —*top/bottom*— of any Chess diagram.

bottom

—60—

In the following frames, we shall assume that you are playing with the White pieces. The squares in the files are numbered away from you, starting with the rank nearest to you. Thus the starting position of your King is called King 1. The square in front of the King is called King 2.

Put an x in the square King 4.

—451—

A Chess game is conventionally divided into three parts:

1. The OPENING, in which the central Pawns, the Knights, and the Bishops are developed (moved out toward the center of the board).

2. The MIDDLE GAME, in which each player struggles for superiority in material and position, and tries to find a way to checkmate his opponent.

3. The END GAME, in which there are only a few pieces left on the board. When only the King remains on one side, the other side must have a superiority of at least a Rook in order to force _____.

checkmate

—452—

It is impossible to force checkmate with only a King and a Knight, or a King and a _____.

In addition, a King and two Knights cannot force checkmate; but a King, a Bishop, and a Knight, or a King and two Bishops can force checkmate.

These forced checkmates are too difficult to examine at this time, but we shall now practice some checkmates in simple end-game situations.

Bishop

—453—

Place the Black King on QB4; place a White Rook on KN4, and the White Queen on KB7.

The Queen and the Rook can easily force a checkmate without the assistance of the White King. They simply force the Black King to the side of the board by cutting off one rank or file after another from him.

∞

—61—

Put an x in Queen 2.

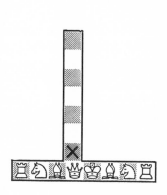

—62—

Put an x in Queen 1.

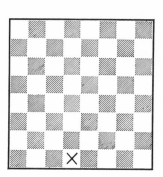

—63—

Put an x in King 3 .

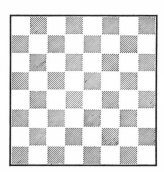

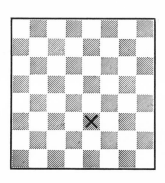

Replace the Black chessmen in the same castled positions. Place the White Queen on KN5, and a White Pawn on KB6.

White threatens _____.

QxNP mate

∞

But it is Black's move.

What is Black's only possible defense? ..._____

...P-KN3

∞

Now White cannot checkmate Black immediately, but the Queen can move to a square from which she will again threaten checkmate. This square is _____.

KR6

∞

White now threatens _____.

Q-KN7 mate

∞

Does Black have any way of preventing this checkmate?

no

∞

Black can move only his _____, _____, and _____.

King, Rook, KNP

∞

The Black King can move only to _____, where he would still be checkmated on the next move.

KR1

∞

The King Knight Pawn can move only to _____, a move which obviously cannot prevent the checkmate.

KN4

∞

The Black Rook can move only along Black's _____ rank; this cannot help the threatened King. Checkmate is inevitable.

first

—64—

Put an x in Queen 7.

—65—

The Bishop next to the King is called the King Bishop. The Knight and Rook on the King side of the board are called the _____ Knight and the _____ Rook.

King, King

—66—

The Bishop next to the Queen is called the _____ Bishop.

Queen

∞

Similarly, the Knight and Rook on the Queen side of the board are called the _____ _____ and the _____ _____.

Queen Knight, Queen Rook

∞

The file on which the Queen Rook stands is called the _____ _____ file.

Queen Rook

Place a White Knight on KN5, and the White Queen on Q3. What move will checkmate Black? _____	QxKRP mate
∞	
Place a White Bishop on KB6, and a White Rook on KN2. How can White checkmate Black with a check followed by a discovered check? _____	RxKNP ch
∞	
Black's only possible move is ..._____.	...K-KR1
∞	
White then plays R-KN5 _____.	mate
∞	
The Rook withdrew to expose the King to a discovered check from the Bishop while still covering Black's KN1, the only square not covered by the _____.	Bishop
∞	
Note that White could as easily have moved the Rook to KN6, or to any of the squares further back on the King Knight file. He had to avoid only KN8 where he would have been captured by the —*Rook/King*.	King
∞	
Why didn't White play RxBP dis ch?	Black could move ...K-KN1.
∞	
Why not RxRP dbl ch?	Black would play ...KxR.
∞	

—67—

The file on which the King Bishop is placed is called the _____ _____ _____.

King Bishop file

∞

Place an x in King Bishop 1.

—68—

Place an x in King Bishop 4.

—69—

Place an x in King Knight 5.

—*450*—

Since your opponent will usually have a chance to castle, many of your opportunities to checkmate him will involve attacks on the position of the castled King.

In order to simplify the situation, we shall use only the Black King in his castled position on the King side, the Rook beside him, the three Pawns which are usually in front of the King and Rook, and the attacking White pieces.

The Black King will therefore go on the square _____.

KN1

∞

The Black Rook will be on _____.

KB1

∞

The three Pawns will be on _____, _____, _____.

KB2, KN2, KR2

∞

In the following examples, we shall always assume that it is White's move. Place a White Rook on KR1, and the White Queen on QB2.

What move will checkmate Black? _____

QxKRP mate

∞

Replace the captured Pawn after this and each of the following checkmates. Then always remove the White pieces from the board. The Black King, Rook, and Pawn formation will remain the same.

∞

Place a White Bishop on QN2, and the White Queen on QB3. What move will checkmate Black? _____

QxKNP mate

∞

Remember to replace the Pawn and to clear the White pieces from the board.

∞

—70—

Place x's in King Rook 4 and in
Queen Bishop 6.

 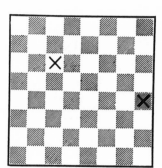

—71—

Place x's in Queen 6 and in King
Knight 2.

—72—

Place x's in Queen Rook 7 and in
King 5.

White	Black

7. B-QN3

Can White castle?   yes

∞

8. O-O	8. P-Q4
9. P-K5	9. N-K5
10. K-KR1	10. Q-KR5
11. NxQP??	

White is wasting time which he needed to move his pieces to the King's side to protect his King.

11. B-KN5

What is Black's threat? _____   ...BxQ

∞

| 12. P-KB3 | 12. N-KN6 ch |

Why can't White play 13. PxN?

He would be exposing his King to check. The Pawn is pinned by the Black Queen.

∞

What is White's only possible move?

13. _____   K-KN1

∞

How can Black win the game with a double check?

13. _____   ...NxKBP mate

∞

Remove all pieces from the board.

—73—

Place x's in Queen Knight 8 and in King Rook 3.

—74—

What square is the White Rook on?

Queen Rook 1

—75—

What square is the White Rook on?

Queen Rook 6

—449—

Replace the pieces in their starting positions, with the Black chessmen on your side of the board. As the following game demonstrates, castling does not necessarily insure the King's safety.

In this game both sides castle, but Black develops his pieces more rapidly, and successfully attacks the castled White King. Make the following moves:

White		Black	
1.	P-K4	1.	P-K4
2.	N-KB3	2.	N-QB3
3.	N-QB3	3.	N-KB3

This opening is called the Four _____ game.

Knights'
_____

∞

4.	B-QN5	4.	N-Q5
5.	NxP	5.	B-QB4
6.	B-QR4		

Can Black castle?

yes
_____

Position after
7. N-Q3?

6.		O-O
7.	N-Q3?	

Check with the diagram.

Queen
Bishop

∞

This move is bad because it blocks White's _____ Pawn. which in turn blocks the diagonal for his Queen _____ .

∞

—76—

What square is the White Rook on?

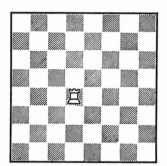

Queen 4

—77—

What square is the White Knight on?

King Knight 3

—78—

What square is the White Knight on?

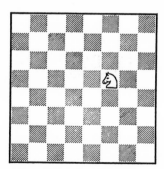

King Bishop 5

	White	Black	

Black plays

9. _____   ...PxQ

∞

Position after
9. ...PxQ

Check with the diagram.

∞

What are the only two moves which will place the Black King in check? _____, _____   B-K6 ch, B-K8 ch

∞

Which of these moves would simply lose the White Bishop? _____   B-K8 ch

∞

White therefore plays

10. _____ ch   B-K6

∞

What is Black's only possible reply?

10. _____   ...K-K1

∞

What move will now checkmate Black?

11. _____   P-KB7 mate

—79—

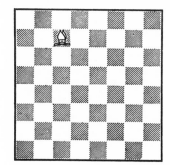

What square is the White Bishop on?

Queen Bishop 7

—80—

What square is the White Queen on?

King Knight 6

—81—

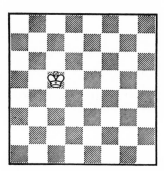

What square is the White King on?

Queen Bishop 5

White	Black	Position after 4. ...KN-K2?
4. O-O	4. KN-K2?	

Check with the diagram.

This move is bad because it blocks the diagonal for Black's Queen and permits White to make the following move:

5. N-KN5	5. P-KB3	

∞

White could now fork Black's Queen and King Rook with his Knight by moving _____, but he prefers to go directly for the checkmate.

N-KB7

∞

6. B-KB7 ch

Black's only possible move is

6. _____   ...K-Q2

∞

What move of the White Queen will now continue the attack?
7. _____   Q-KN4 ch

∞

| 7. | P-KB4 | |
| 8. PxP | 8. P-KR4 | |

Black tries to stop White's mating threat by attacking his Queen.

Now, how can White continue his attack with a discovered check?

9. _____   P-KB6 dis ch

∞

In order to force checkmate, White has given up his Queen. This is an example of a Queen _____.   sacrifice

∞

—82—

You are now ready to learn the abbreviations for the names of the pieces. The abbreviation for King is K.

The abbreviation for Queen must be ____.

Q

—83—

The abbreviation for Rook is ____.

R

∞

The abbreviation for Bishop is ____.

B

—84—

____ is the abbreviation for Pawn.

P

—85—

To avoid confusion with the abbreviation for King, the abbreviation used for Knight is N.

The abbreviation QN must mean _____ _____.

Queen Knight

∞

The abbreviation KN must mean _____ _____.

King Knight

—86—

The abbreviation KR must mean _____ _____.

King Rook

Move the Black Rook to QB1. Can White castle?

no

∞

Why not?

The Black Rook covers the square to which the King moves. He would be castling into check.

∞

It is helpful to remember that in castling the King moves sideward left or right to the nearest square of the same color. Then the _____ toward which he moved is brought around to the square on the other side of the King.

Rook

∞

Castling is permanently impossible if the _____ or the _____ on the side toward which you wish to castle has been moved.

King
Rook

∞

The abbreviation for CASTLES KING SIDE is O-O. O-O-O means CASTLES _____ SIDE.

QUEEN

—448—

The following game is a vivid illustration of what can happen when one player develops his pieces well and castles, and the other player does not. Make the following moves:

	White		Black
1.	P-K4	1.	P-K4
2.	N-KB3	2.	N-QB3
3.	B-QB4	3.	P-Q3?

This is a bad move because it blocks the diagonal for Black's _____ _____.

King Bishop

∞

—87—

The abbreviation QB must mean _____ _____ .

Queen Bishop

—88—

Write the abbreviation for Queen Knight. _____

QN

—89—

Write the abbreviation for Queen Rook. _____

QR

—90—

Write the abbreviation for King Bishop. _____

KB

—91—

Write the abbreviation for King Knight. _____

KN

—92—

Fill in the abbreviations for the pieces in the blanks beneath the symbols.

QR QN QB Q K KB KN KR

Castle Queen side and check with the diagram.

∞

Notice that the major difference is that the Rook has moved over _____ squares, whereas it moved only _____ squares when you castled King side.

three
two

∞

The same rules apply to castling Queen side. You cannot castle if your _____ or your _____ has been previously moved.

King, Rook

∞

You cannot castle if your King is ____ _____, or if the square he moves over or the square he lands on is covered by an _____ piece.

in check

enemy

∞

Replace the King on K1 and the Rook on QR1. Place a Black Rook on Q1. Can White castle?

no

∞

Why not?

The Black Rook covers the square Q1 over which the White King must pass.

∞

Move the Black Rook to QN1. Now can White castle?

yes

∞

—93—

Henceforth you will always use the abbreviations which you have learned to describe the positions of the pieces on the chessboard. Thus if a chessman is on Queen 2, we abbreviate this position Q2.

Write the abbreviation for the position of the White Knight. _____

K6

—94—

Write the abbreviation for the position of the White Rook. _____

Q3

—95—

Write the abbreviation for the position of the White Bishop. _____

KN5

∞

Write the abbreviation for the position of the White Knight. _____

QR4

Move the Black Bishop to QB5. Now can White castle?	no
∞	
Why not?	The Bishop covers the square over which the King must pass.
∞	
Move the Black Bishop to K5. Now can White castle?	yes
∞	
Why?	The King is not *in check*; the Bishop covers neither the square upon which he *lands* nor the square over which he must *pass*.
∞	
Remove the pieces from the board.	

—447—

You have just practiced castling King side. It is also possible, although much less common, to castle Queen side.

Here again, you move your King two squares, but this time it is two squares to the left. You then move your Rook around him. So the King moves to the square _____.

QB1

∞

And the Queen Rook moves to the square _____.

Q1

∞

—96—

Write the abbreviation for the position of the White Queen. _____

∞

Write the abbreviation for the position of the White Pawn. _____

KR4

—————

KB5

—97—

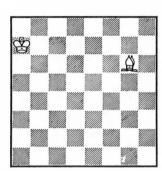

Write the abbreviation for the position of the White King. _____

∞

Write the abbreviation for the position of the White Bishop. _____

QR7

—————

KN6

—98—

Each chessman has its special way of moving. You will now learn how to move your King. The King moves in any direction, one square at a time. Thus he can move one square forward, backward, sideward, or diagonally.

The White King is on _____.

∞

The x's in the adjacent squares show that he has _____ possible moves.

Q5

—————

8

Observe the positions of the chessmen.

Can White castle?

no

_____

∞

Why not?

His Rook has been moved.

_____

∞

Replace the White King on K1 and the Rook on KR1. Here is another rule about castling: you cannot castle if the King is in check, or if the square that he moves over or the square he lands on is covered by an enemy piece.

Place a Black Bishop on QN5. Can White castle?

no

_____

Why not?

The King is in check.

_____

∞

Move the Black Bishop to Q5. Now can White castle?

no

_____

∞

Why not?

The Bishop covers the square on which the King lands. Note that this rule seems natural enough, because the King would be moving into check.

∞

—99—

The King is on _____.

KN4

∞

Draw x's in all the squares to which he might possibly move.

—100—

With no other pieces on the chessboard, place the King on K1. Can he move to K2?

yes

∞

Can the King move from K1 to Q2?

yes

∞

Starting from K1, the King can move to —Q3/KB1.

KB1

—101—

Place the King on QN5. Can he move to QB4?

yes

—102—

no

Place the King on KN3. Can he move to KN1?

—446—

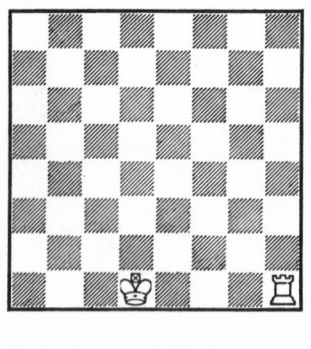

Place the White King on K1, and a White Rook on KR1. Castle and check with the diagram to see that you have done it correctly.

∞

Replace the King on K1 and the Rook on KR1. Place a Knight on KN1. Now can White castle?

no

∞

Why not?

There is a piece between the King and the Rook.

∞

Remove the Knight, and place a Bishop on KB1. Can White castle?

no

∞

Observe the positions of the chessmen.

Can White castle?

no

∞

Why not?

His King has been moved.

∞

—103—

Underline the correct answers: The King can move one square (1) forward, (2) backward, (3) sideward, (4) diagonally.

forward, backward, sideward, diagonally (All are correct.)

—104—

The White Queen is on _____.

K4

∞

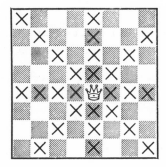

Like the King, the Queen moves forward, backward, sideward, and diagonally. There is one great difference, however, between the moves of the King and the Queen. Whereas the King can move only _____ square in any direction, the Queen can move any distance in a straight line.

one

∞

Can the Queen in the diagram move to any square marked with an x?

yes

—105—

The White Queen is on _____.

Q5

∞

Mark with x's all the squares to which the Queen might possibly move.

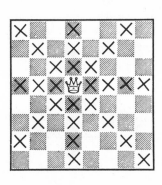

So White does not play P-Q3. Instead of this, White CASTLES.

Castling is a special move to protect your King. It is the only time in Chess that you are allowed to move two pieces at once. These two pieces are your King and your Rook.

Move the White King over two squares to the right to KN1. Now move the KR to the left around the King to KB1. You have just castled.

Check with the diagram to be sure that you have done it correctly.

∞

It is now Black's move. He is also in a position to castle. Make this move for Black and check with the diagram to be sure that you have done it correctly.

∞

Note that castling not only protects your King by getting him away from the center of the board to a place where he is protected by a wall of Pawns, but also moves your _____ nearer to the center, where it can take a more active part in the game.

Rook

∞

There are several limitations placed upon castling. Obviously you cannot castle if there are any pieces between your _____ and your Rook. And you cannot castle if you have previously moved either your King or your Rook.

King

∞

Remove all pieces from the board so that you can practice castling.

—106—

With no other pieces on the board, place the White Queen on QB4. Can the Queen move to QB8?

yes
(The Queen can move any distance forward.)

—107—

Place the White Queen on Q3. Can she move to QN5?

yes
(The Queen can move any distance diagonally.)

—108—

Place the White Queen on KN3. Can she move to QB3?

yes
(The Queen can move any distance sideward.)

—109—

Place the White Queen on KR7. Can she move to KR2?

yes
(The Queen can move any distance backward.)

—110—

Place the White Queen on Q4. Can she move to KR2?

∞

Remove the Queen from the board.

no
(The Queen can move only in straight lines.)

—111—

Place the White King on K5. Can the King move to KN7?

∞

Remove the King from the board.

no
(The King can move only one square at a time.)

—445—

The King is in great danger if left in the middle of the board. In the following game you will learn a new way to protect him.

Here are the first four moves in an opening called the FOUR KNIGHTS' GAME. They illustrate a basic general principle in Chess. After your initial Pawn move, you should move your Knights from their starting positions first, then your Bishops.

As you learn more about Chess, you will see how you can safely vary this procedure, but it is a good general rule for beginners. Moving your chessmen from their starting positions out onto the board is called DEVELOPING your pieces.

You develop first your Knights, and then your _____.

Bishops

∞

Make the following moves:

	White		Black
1.	P-K4	1.	P-K4
2.	N-KB3	2.	N-QB3
3.	N-QB3	3.	N-KB3
4.	B-QN5	4.	B-QN5

Position after
4. ...B-QN5

Check with the diagram.

∞

The fact that White's King is still in the center of the board is already beginning to cause him trouble. If he plays P-Q3 in order to develop his QB, his Knight on QB3 will be pinned by the Black Bishop on QN5. Why couldn't White then move the Knight?

His King would be in check.

∞

—112—

The White Rook is on _____.

Q5

∞

Like the _____, the Rook can move any distance forward, backward, or sideward. Thus the Rook can move to any of the squares marked x.

Queen

∞

Unlike the Queen, however, the Rook cannot move _____.

diagonally

—113—

The White _____ is on _____.

Rook
KB3

∞

Mark with x's all the squares to which the Rook can move.

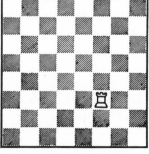

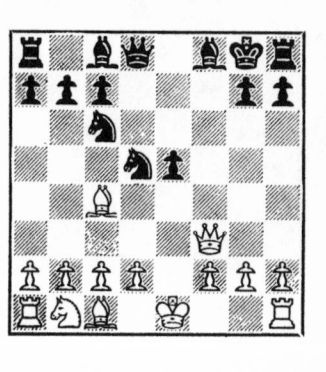

Black, however, does not realize this. He abandons his Knight, and hopes to protect his King by moving 7. ...K-KN1. Make this move and check with the diagram.

∞

White can now win by capturing the Knight with either the Queen or the Bishop. He chooses to play 8. QxN ch.

Black cannot move his King. He must either _____ the Queen or _____ his Queen Bishop.

capture
interpose

∞

He plays 8. ...QxQ.

White then plays 9. _____

BxQ ch

∞

Now Black can neither move his King nor capture the checking Bishop. His only possible move is 9. ..._____

...B-K3
(interposing the
Bishop)

∞

White's next move is 10. _____

BxB mate

∞

Replace all the chessmen in their starting positions.

—114—

With no other pieces on the board, place a White Rook on KN6. Can the Rook move to KB6?

yes

—115—

In the following frames, you will practice moving your Rook, King and Queen. At the end of each frame, remove the piece you are using from the board.

Place a White Rook on Q4. Can it move to QB5?

no
(The Rook cannot move diagonally.)

—116—

Place a White Rook on QR2. Can it move to QR7?

yes

—117—

Place the White King on Q6. Can he move to Q8?

no
(The King can move only one square at a time.)

—118—

Place the White Queen on KB6. Can she move to QR1?

yes

Why didn't Black capture the Pawn with the Queen?

∞

White must do something about his Knight on KN5, or it will be captured by the Black _____.

∞

White decides on a clever sacrifice. He plays 6. NxKBP.

This is a speculative exchange because White is giving up a Knight for a Pawn. Hence it is called a _____.

∞

In Chess, you sacrifice either with the hope of regaining your material and more from a superior position, or, very often, in order to force a checkmate.

What move will Black now make? 6. ..._____

∞

The Knight on Q4 is now _____ by the White Bishop.

∞

White plays 7. Q-KB3 ch, simultaneously checking the King and attacking the Black _____ on _____.

∞

The Knight is now attacked by both the White Bishop and the White Queen, and defended only by the Black Queen. Black must move his King out of check. What is the only move which will simultaneously defend his Knight and get his King out of check? ..._____

∞

White would have captured the Queen with the Bishop.

_____

Queen

_____

sacrifice

_____

...KxN

_____

pinned

_____

Knight
Q4

_____

...K-K3

—119—

The White Bishop is on _____.

K3

∞

The Bishop can move to any of the squares marked with an x.

Can the Bishop move straight forward, backward or sideward?

no

∞

Like the Queen, the Bishop can move any distance, but unlike the Queen, the Bishop moves only _____.

diagonally

—120—

The Rook can move any distance forward, backward or _____, but the Rook cannot move_____.

sideward
diagonally

∞

The _____ can move only diagonally.

Bishop

This means that if White captures the Pawn, he would exchange his Bishop for a Pawn. Is this a good exchange for White?

no

∞

Therefore the Black Pawn is in no immediate danger. Black plays 3. ...N-KB3, attacking White's KP.

White moves 4. N-KN5. This move not only defends the KP but also attacks Black's KBP.

Position after
4. N-KN5

Check with the diagram.

∞

What is White's threat?

NxKBP
(forking the Black
Queen and the KR)

∞

In this case, Black will not be able to capture the Knight because the Pawn is defended only by the King, and the King cannot move _____ _____.

into check
(from the White
Bishop)

∞

Black finds a good way to defend the Pawn.
He moves 4. ...P-Q4.

White moves 5. PxP.

How will Black recapture the Pawn? 5. ..._____.

...NxP

∞

—121—

The White _____ is on _____.

Bishop
QB4

∞

Mark with x's all the squares to which the Bishop can move.

—122—

Place a White Bishop on KN2. Can it move to KN3?

no
(The Bishop moves only diagonally. It cannot move forward, sideward or backward.)

—123—

Place a White Bishop on Q4. Can it move to KR8?

yes

—124—

Place a White Bishop on Q2. This is a —black/white— square.

black

∞

Will this Bishop ever be able to move to a white square?

no

—443—

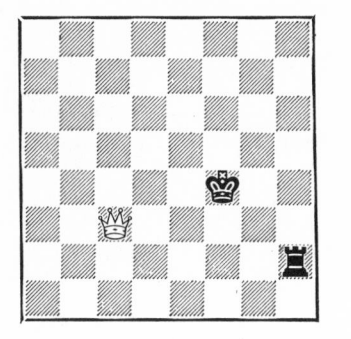

What move will win the Black Rook? _____

Q-QB7 ch

—444—

Set up the pieces in their starting positions, with the White chessmen on your side of the board.

White moves 1. P-K4.

This move opens up diagonals for White's _____ and his King _____.

Queen
Bishop

∞

What is a likely reply for Black? 1. ..._____

...P-K4

∞

White moves 2. N-KB3, attacking Black's KP. What Knight move will defend this Pawn? 2. ..._____

...N-QB3

∞

White moves 3. B-QB4.

This Bishop is attacking Black's _____.

KBP

∞

What Black piece is defending this Pawn?

the King

∞

—125—

Place one White Bishop on KB1 and the other on QB1. The King Bishop is on a _____ square; the Queen Bishop is on a _____ square.

white
black

∞

Will the King Bishop always move on the white squares?

yes

∞

The Queen Bishop will always move on the _____ squares.

black

—126—

The King moves one square _____, _____, _____, or _____.

forward, backward, sideward, diagonally

—127—

The Queen moves any distance _____, _____, _____, or _____.

forward, backward, sideward, diagonally

—128—

A Rook moves any distance _____, _____, or _____.

forward, backward, sideward

—129—

A Bishop moves any distance _____.

diagonally

Black has to move his King out of check, and White's next move is _____.

RxQ

—441—

What move will win the Black Queen? _____

B-QN3 ch

—442—

Place the Black King on KB5, and the Black Queen on KN5; place a White Rook on Q8. What move will win the Black Queen? _____

R-Q4 ch

∞

The Black King will move to a square —*adjacent to*/ *away from*— the Black Queen.

adjacent to

∞

Why?

The King will then be in a position to capture the Rook on the next move.

—130—

Place a White Rook on KR1. Can it move to KN2?

no
(The Rook cannot move diagonally.)

—131—

Place the White King on QN4. Can he move to QB5?

yes
(The King can move one square forward, backward, sideward, or diagonally.)

—132—

Place the White Queen on K1. Can she move to QN1?

yes
(The Queen can move any distance forward, backward, sideward, or diagonally.)

—133—

The Queen, _____ and _____ have moves of varying lengths. The Knight has a move of fixed length.

Rook, Bishop

—134—

This diagram illustrates a move of the Knight:

This Knight has moved one square straight _____ and then one square _____ to the right. This constitutes one Knight move.

forward
diagonally

—439—

Make the following moves:

	White		Black
1.	P-Q4	1.	N-KB3
2.	P-QB4	2.	P-K4
3.	P-Q5	3.	B-QB4
4.	B-KN5??		

Check with the diagram.

∞

The White Bishop has _____ the Black Knight.

∞

If Black moves the pinned Knight, he will lose his Queen. Usually it is good practice to rely on a pin, but in this case White has forgotten to defend his King. Black moves

4.   N-K5

5.   BxQ

What move will checkmate White?

5.   _____

∞

The Black Knight covers White's _____, the King's only possible escape square.

—440—

Another good way to win material is a sort of reverse pin called an X-RAY or SKEWER.

Place the Black King on K4, and the Black Queen on QN4; place a White Rook on KR1. What move will win the Black Queen? _____

∞

Position after
4. B-KN5

pinned

...BxP mate

Q2

R-KR5 ch

—135—

Here is another possible move of the Knight:

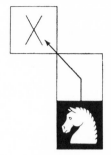

This time the Knight has moved one square straight forward and then one square _____ to the _____.

diagonally
left

—136—

Here is still another possible move of the Knight:

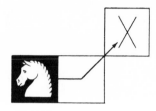

The Knight has moved one square straight sideward and then one square _____.

diagonally

—137—

Draw an arrow to show the move of the Knight.

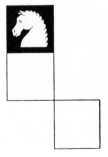

∞

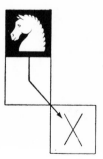

The Knight has moved one square straight _____ and then one square _____.

backward
diagonally

—438—

Set up the pieces in their starting positions, with the Black chessmen on your side of the board. Make the following moves:

White	Black
1. P-K4	1. P-K4
2. P-Q4	2. PxP
3. QxP?	

Check with the diagram.

∞

Except in rare cases, such as the Fool's Mate which you have already learned, it is very bad practice to bring your Queen out on the board early in the opening. If you do, your opponent will gain time by driving your Queen around the board with his Knights and Bishops. What Knight move will now attack the White Queen?

3. _____   ...N-QB3

∞

White has to move his Queen. He plays

4. Q-QB3??

The Queen should have moved to K3 where she would be temporarily out of danger.

What move will now win the White Queen?

4. _____   ...B-QN5

∞

The Queen is now _____ by the Black Bishop.   pinned

∞

If she moved off the diagonal, the King would be in check.

Hence White has lost his _____, and is well on his way to losing the game.   Queen

∞

Replace the chessmen in their starting positions.

—138—

Draw arrows to show the possible moves of the Knight.

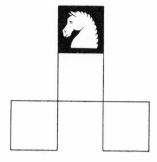

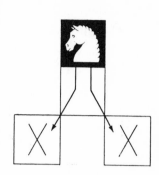

—139—

Draw arrows to show the possible moves of the Knight.

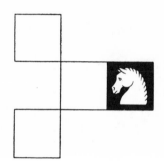

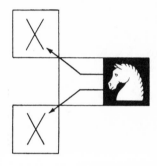

—140—

A Knight moves one square forward, backward, or sideward, and then one square _____.

diagonally

Arrows have been drawn to show two of the possible moves of the Knight. Draw arrows to show the other six.

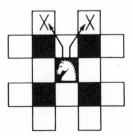

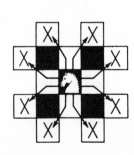

—435—

What move will win the Black Queen? _____

B-K1

—436—

If aided by another piece, a Rook can also pin the Queen. Place the Black King on Q1, and the Black Queen on Q4; place a White Rook on QR3, and a White Knight on KB2.

What move will win the Black Queen? _____

R-Q3

—437—

Place the Black King on QB2, and the Black Queen on K4; place the White Queen on KR4, and the White Bishop on K1. What move will win the Black Queen? _____

B-KN3

∞

Why not Q-KN3?

This would merely force an even exchange of Queens.

—141—

The White Knight is on _____.

K5

∞

The Knight moves one square forward, backward, or sideward, and then one more square _____, but continuing in a direction away from his starting square.

diagonally

∞

The x's on the diagram show the ____ possible moves of the Knight.

8

—142—

The White _____ is on _____.

Knight
KB3

∞

The Knight can move to any one of ____ squares.

8

∞

Mark with x's the squares to which the Knight can move.

—433—

What move will win the Black Knight? _____

R-QR5

∞

The Knight is _____ in front of the King.

pinned

—434—

An unaided Bishop or Rook cannot pin the Queen in front of the King because the Queen would simply _____ the attacking piece.

capture

∞

Place the Black King on KR1, and the Black Queen on K4; place a White Bishop on QB1.

If White moves B-QN2, trying to pin the Black Queen in front of the King, Black will then play ..._____.

...QxB

∞

But if we add a White Rook on QN7, White will win the Black Queen in exchange for his Bishop. A Bishop can _____ the opponent's Queen in front of the King only if aided by a friendly piece.

pin

—143—

Place a White Knight on QB5. This is a _____ square. If the Knight starts on a black square, he will always move to a _____ square.

black

white

—144—

Place a White Knight on K6. From this position the Knight can move only to _____ squares.

black

—145—

Place a White Knight on QN5. Can it move to QB7?

yes
(The Knight has moved one square straight forward, and then one square diagonally to the right.)

—146—

Place a White Knight on Q3. Can it move to KB4?

yes
(The Knight has moved one square straight sideward, and then one square diagonally to the left.)

—147—

Place a White Knight on QR4. Can it move to QR6?

no

∞

The Knight cannot move two squares straight forward. It can move only one square forward, and then must move one square_____ to the_____ or to the_____ .

diagonally
right, left

What move will pin the Black Rook? _____

B-QB3

∞

Why mustn't Black move the Rook?

White would play BxQ.

—431—

The Bishop can pin one of two Rooks in much the same way. Place one Black Rook on KR7, and the other Black Rook on K4. Place the White Bishop on Q8. What move will win a Rook? _____

B-QB7

∞

The Rook nearest to the Bishop is _____ because if it is moved White will capture the other Rook.

pinned

∞

If Black moves the further Rook, can White capture the nearer one?

yes

—432—

How can White pin the Black Bishop? _____

R-K1

—148—

Place a White Knight on KR1. What are the two possible squares to which the Knight can move? _____ _____

KN3, KB2

—149—

Place a White Knight on QR8. What are the two squares to which the Knight can move? _____ _____

QN6, QB7

—150—

The Knight is the only one of the chessmen that can jump over the other pieces.

In the diagram, the White Knight on _____ is completely surrounded by White and Black pieces.

Q4

Can the Knight move to QB6?

yes

Can he move to K2?

yes

Can he move to Q3?

no

Mark with x's all the squares to which the White Knight can move.

Place the Black King on KN2, and a Black Rook on Q5; place a White Bishop on K1. White moves B-QB3, attacking the Black Rook. Can the Rook move?

no

∞

Why not?

Any move of the Rook exposes the King to check.

∞

Therefore Black cannot move his Rook, and the White Bishop will capture it on the next move.

—428—

What move will pin the Black Rook? _____

B-KB5

—429—

Place the Black King on KN8, and a Black Knight on Q5; place a White Bishop on QR3. What move will win the Black Knight? _____

B-QB5

∞

Why can't the Knight move?

The Black King would be in check.

—430—

When a Bishop pins a piece in front of the Queen, it is legal for the piece to move away, but it is almost unthinkable because such a move gives up the Queen.

∞

—151—

Now it is a White Bishop on Q4, completely surrounded by other pieces.

Can the White Bishop move to QR1?

no

∞

Can the Bishop move to KN7?

no

∞

Can the Bishop move to KB2?

no
(The Bishop cannot jump over other chessmen.)

—152—

Now a Rook is in the position formerly occupied by the Bishop.

Can the Rook move to Q8?

no

∞

Can it move to KR4?

no
(The Rook cannot jump over other chessmen.)

Is a Queen worth more than a Knight and a Bishop?	yes
∞	
Which is worth more, two Bishops, or a Rook?	two Bishops
∞	
Which is worth more, a Queen, or a Knight and a Rook?	a Queen
∞	
Which is worth more, a Bishop, or four Pawns?	four Pawns
∞	
Which is worth more, a Queen, or two Knights and a Bishop?	They are equal.
∞	
Which is worth more, a Rook, or a Knight and three Pawns?	A Knight and three Pawns.

∞

Now that you know the value of the pieces, you should be on the watch for situations where you can exchange chessmen of little value for those of greater value.

—427—

A PIN is one of the most common ways of winning material. A piece is pinned when it cannot move without exposing a more valuable chessman to attack. This more valuable piece is often the King or the Queen, but it may be a Rook, Knight or Bishop. Usually a Bishop does the pinning.

∞

—153—

Now it is the Queen that is surrounded.

Can the Queen jump over any of
the other White or Black pieces to
reach the squares beyond them?

no

—154—

The _____ is the only piece that can jump over the
other chess pieces.

Knight

—155—

A Rook moves any distance _____, _____
or _____.

forward, backward,
sideward

∞

The White _____ is on _____.

Rook
QN3

∞

If the Black Queen then captures the White Knight, will White have gained material?

∞

| | yes |

Why?

| | The Rook is worth more than the Knight. |

_____

—426—

You will now learn the exact values of the chessmen. You already know that the _____ is the most powerful piece on the board.

∞

| | Queen |

The second most powerful piece is the _____.

∞

| | Rook |

The _____ and the _____ are of equal value.

∞

| | Knight, Bishop |

The _____ is the weakest of the chessmen.

∞

| | Pawn |

But when you exchange a Queen for a Knight and a Bishop, or for a Rook and a Knight, you will want to know whether you have won or lost material.

Here is a table of values which will give a clearer idea of the relative worth of the chessmen. No value is assigned to the King since he, of course, cannot be exchanged.

Queen	9
Rook	5
Bishop	3
Knight	3
Pawn	1

Learn these relative values of the pieces so that you can answer questions such as the following:

∞

Mark with x's all the squares to which the Rook might move.

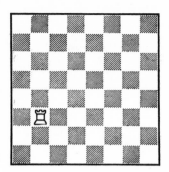

A Knight moves one square _____, _____, or _____ and then one square _____, but continuing in the direction _____ from its starting square.

forward, backward, sideward
diagonally
away

∞

The White _____ is on ____.

Knight
KB4

∞

Mark with x's all the squares to which the Knight can move.

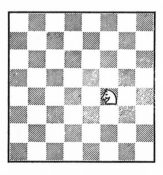

—424—

We shall now review some useful ways of gaining material which you have already learned, and shall then practice some new ones.

How can White win a piece?_____

P-Q4

∞

This is called a Pawn _____.

fork

∞

Since it is the more valuable of his two pieces, Black will move the _____ away.

Rook

∞

Will White then capture the Knight?

yes

—425—

How can White win material with a Knight fork? _____

N-K5

∞

Black will move away his _____, and White will capture the _____ on his next move.

Queen
Rook

∞

—157—

A Bishop moves any distance _____.

diagonally

∞

The White _____ is on ____.

Bishop
Q4

∞

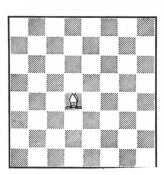

Mark with x's all the squares to which the Bishop can move.

—158—

The Queen moves any distance_____, _____, _____ or _____.

forward, backward, sideward, diagonally

∞

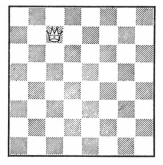

The White _____ is on ____.

Queen
QB7

∞

—423—

Here is a game in which Black forces an early checkmate by "smothering" the Queen.

Make the following moves:

	White		Black
1.	P-Q4	1.	N-KB3
2.	N-Q2	2.	P-K4
3.	PxP	3.	N-KN5
4.	P-KR3??		

White tries to drive away the Knight, but this move is a mistake which costs him the game.

4.   N-K6

What is the only move which will save the smothered White Queen?

5.   _____   PxN

∞

Note that White now has tripled Pawns on his King file. The move 5. PxN saves his Queen, but loses the game to a forced checkmate. What move will now check the White King?

5.   _____   ...Q-KR5 ch

∞

What is White's only possible move?

6.   _____   P-KN3

∞

What move will checkmate White?

6.   _____   ...QxKNP mate

∞

This checkmate is similar to the _____ Mate which we met earlier.   Fool's

Mark with x's all the squares to which the Queen can move.

—159—

The King moves one square _____, _____, _____ or _____.

forward, backward, sideward, diagonally

∞

The White _____ is on _____.

King
QN2

∞

Mark with x's all the squares to which the King can move.

Why can't he capture the White Pawn?

He would be moving into check from the White Bishop.

—422—

The Queen can also be "smothered" by a Knight. Set up the pieces in their starting positions with the White chessmen on your side of the board. Make the following moves:

	White		Black
1.	P-K4	1.	P-Q3
2.	B-QB4	2.	N-Q2
3.	N-KB3	3.	P-KN3
4.	N-KN5		

What is White's threat? _____

BxKBP mate

∞

Black plays   4.   N-KR3

Does this move prevent the checkmate?

yes

∞

---

5.   BxP ch

What is Black's only possible move?

5.   _____

...NxB

∞

What move will now win the Black Queen?

6.   _____

N-K6
(The Queen is the victim of a smothered attack.)

∞

Replace the chessmen in their starting positions.

—160—

The White Pawn is on _____.

K4

The Pawn moves only one square in one direction -- straight forward. An x marks the only square to which the Pawn can move.

—161—

The White _____ is on _____.

Pawn
KN6

∞

Mark with an x the only square to which the Pawn can move.

—419—

It is White's move.

What move will checkmate the Black King? _____

N-QB7 mate

—420—

When a Knight places the opponent's King in check and the King cannot move because all of the adjoining squares are occupied by his own pieces, this is called a _____ _____.

smothered mate

—421—

Other White pieces can also take part in a smothered mate of the Black King if the King cannot capture them without moving into check.

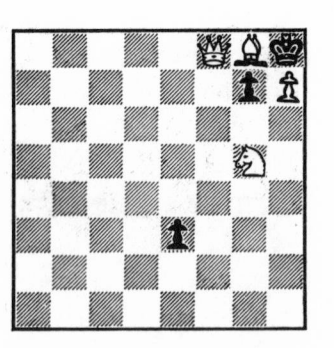

It is White's move.

What move will checkmate the Black King? _____

N-KB7 mate

∞

Why can't the Black King capture the White Bishop?

He would be moving into check from the White Queen and Pawn.

∞

—162—

Place a White Pawn on QB5. What is the only square to which this Pawn can move? _____

QB6

∞

Pawns can never move backward.
They can move only straight _____.

forward

—163—

With no other pieces on the board, place a White Pawn on KN4. Can the Pawn move to KN6?

no
(The Pawn moves only one square at a time.)

—164—

When a Pawn reaches the eighth rank (corresponding to the King row in Checkers), it can be replaced by any other chessman of its own color (except a King).

The Queen is the strongest piece on the chessboard. Therefore the Pawn is almost always replaced by a _____.

Queen

—165—

Replacing a Pawn with a Queen is called QUEENING.
A Pawn queens when it reaches the _____ rank.

eighth

—166—

Place a White Pawn on KR7. Where must the Pawn move to queen? _____.

KR8

∞

Remove the Pawn from KR8, and replace it with a White _____, as you would in an actual game.

Queen

—*418*—

A draw by perpetual check is usually forced by the Queen. Other pieces can, however, force such a draw.

Place the Black King on KR1, a Black Bishop on KN1, a Black Knight on KN2, and a Black Pawn on KR3; place a White Knight on KB4.

Why should White wish to force a draw?

Black is ahead in material.

_____

∞

What is White's first move in forcing this draw? _____

N-KN6 ch

_____

∞

Then Black moves ..._____.

...K-KR2

_____

∞

And White moves _____.

N-KB8 ch

_____

∞

And Black moves ..._____.

...K-KR1

_____

∞

Why not ...K-KN3?

The King would still be in check from the Knight.

_____

∞

White then moves _____.

N-KN6 ch, etc.

_____

∞

And the position is a _____ by_____ _____.

draw
perpetual check

—167—

As you have already learned, the player of White numbers all the squares from his side of the board. But the player of Black numbers the squares from his side of the board.

This means that the square which is K8 for White's moves is K1 for Black's moves. Black's Q8 is White's _____.

Q1

∞

Black's KR1 is White's _____.

KR8

—168—

White's K4 is Black's _____.

K5

∞

White's Q6 is Black's _____.

Q3

∞

Do the two numbers for the same square always add up to 9?

yes

—169—

White's QN2 is Black's _____.

QN7

∞

Black's KB4 is White's _____.

KB5

—417—

It is White's move. Can he draw the game by perpetual check?

yes

∞

_____

His first move is _____.

Q-Q8 ch

∞

_____

Black's only possible move is ..._____.

...K-QR2

∞

_____

White then moves _____.

Q-QR5 ch

∞

_____

Since Black can still neither _____ a piece nor _____ the Queen, he must move ..._____.

interpose
capture
...K-QN1

∞

_____

White then moves _____.

Q-Q8 ch, etc.

—170—

Henceforth, in setting up the board, we shall place all the White chessmen on their squares from the viewpoint of the player of White, and all the Black chessmen from the viewpoint of the player of Black.

Now, assuming the viewpoint of the player of Black, place the Black King on K1, place Black Pawns on KN2 and KR2, place a Black Knight on KB3 and a Black Bishop on QB4. Check with the diagram to see that you have set up these pieces correctly.

∞

Always remove the pieces from the board at the end of a frame unless you are told to leave them set up.

—171—

If a chessman moves to the square occupied by an opponent's chessman, the opponent's chessman is removed from the board. In Chess this is called CAPTURING.

You _____ an opposing chessman by moving one of your chessmen to the square which it occupies, and removing the hostile chessman from the board.

capture

—172—

White chessmen capture only Black chessmen; Black chessmen capture only _____ chessmen.

White

—173—

Removing an opponent's chessman from the board is called _____.

capturing

All chessmen except the Pawn capture the same way that they move.

—416—

Place the Black King on KR7, a Black Pawn on KR6, a Black Bishop on KR4, the Black Queen on KR1, and a Black Rook on QN1; place the White Queen on QR7.

(Remember that we always assume that the White King is somewhere out of play in all of these examples.)

Black is far ahead in material. White is interested in forcing a draw by _____ _____.

perpetual check

∞

White's first move is _____

Q-KB2 ch

∞

Can Black capture the White Queen or interpose a piece?

no

∞

He must therefore move ..._____.

...K-KR8

∞

White's next move will be _____.

Q-KB1 ch

∞

Black must then move ..._____.

...K-KR7

∞

And White will play _____.

Q-KB2 ch, etc.

—174—

The King _____ the same way that he moves.

captures

—175—

Place the White King on K1 and a Black Knight on K7. Then check with the diagram.

∞

Can the King capture the Knight?

yes

∞

In order to _____ the Knight, move the King from White's K1 to White's K2, the square occupied by the Knight. Remove the Knight from the chessboard.

capture

∞

The King _____ the Knight.

captured

—176—

Place the White King on his QB2 and the Black Knight on his Q6. Can the King capture the Knight?

yes
(The White King moves to Q3 and displaces the Black Knight. The Knight is removed from the board.)

—415—

Place the Black King on QR1, and a Black Rook on QN1; place the White Queen on K2. It is White's move. What move will checkmate Black? _____

| Q-QR6 mate |

∞

Why not Q-QR2 ch?

| The King could move to QN2 where he would be out of check. |

∞

Leave the Black King on QR1. Replace the White Queen on K2, and move the Black Rook to QB1.

It is White's move. What would be the first move of a draw by perpetual check? _____

| Q-QR6 ch |

∞

What is Black's next move? ..._____

| ...K-QN1 |

∞

What is White's next move? _____

| Q-QN6 ch |

∞

What is Black's next move? ..._____

| ...K-QR1 |

∞

And White, of course, moves Q-QR6 ch, etc.

—177—

How many Black pieces are in a position to be captured by the White King?

∞

The symbol for the word "captures" is an "x." Thus King captures Rook is symbolized "KxR." Make the move KxR and check your position with the diagram.

three
(The King can capture the Rook, the Bishop, or the Knight. But remember that he can move only once, and can capture only one of these chessmen at a time.)

—178—

Place the White King on KB3 and a Black Bishop on KN6. Make the following move: KxB.

The _____ has been captured and removed from the board.

(Black) Bishop

∞

The _____ is now on KN3.

(White) King

—179—

Place the White Queen on QN4 and a Black Knight on K2. Can you make the following move: QxN?

yes

With the Queen on KN6, what is the Black King's only move? ..._____

...K-KR1

∞

Where will White move his Queen? _____

Q-KR6 ch

∞

Why not Q-KR5 ch?

The Black King could escape via KN2.

∞

Can the Black King ever escape from these continual checks if White doesn't choose to let him?

no

∞

Therefore the game is a _____ through perpetual check.

draw

∞

It would be foolish of White to force a draw when he is ahead in material. The Queen is worth twice as much as the Black Rook. Add a Black Rook on QR1, a Black Knight on QN1, and the Black Queen on QB1. Black is now far ahead in material. Can he do anything to prevent the perpetual check?

no

∞

None of Black's pieces can _____ the White Queen.

capture

∞

And Black can't _____ any of his pieces between his King and the White Queen.

interpose

∞

Therefore Black's only solution is to continue to move his King out of check.

The game is a draw by _____ _____.

perpetual check

—180—

With the White Queen on QN4 and the Black Knight on K2, add the following pieces to the board: a Black Bishop on K5 and a Black Rook on K8. Underline whichever of the following moves are possible:

(1) QxN   (2) QxB   (3) QxR

∞

Leave the pieces in the same positions.

(1) QxN   (2) QxB   (3) QxR
(All three moves are possible. The Queen can capture any one of the three pieces.)

___

—181—

Add a Black Pawn on KR5.
Is the following move possible: QxP?

∞

White has only one move, and the Queen can capture only one chessman at a time. The Queen —*can*/*cannot*— jump over the Black Bishop in order to capture the Black Pawn.

no

cannot

___

—182—

Place the White Queen on KR8 and a Black Knight on KR7. Is the following move possible: QxN?

yes

___

—183—

Place the White King on K3 and the Black Queen on K4. Is the following move possible: KxQ?

no
(The King can move only one square at a time.)

___

—184—

Place a White Bishop on Q2 and a Black Rook on KR3. Is the following move possible: BxR?

yes
(The Bishop captures the same way that it moves -- diagonally.)

—414—

Place the Black King on KR1, and the White Queen on KN6. It is Black's move. The position is a _____.

stalemate

∞

Is the King in check?

no

∞

Can the King move without moving into check?

no

∞

The game is a _____.

draw

∞

Leaving the King and the Queen in this position, add a Black Rook on KB1. Is the position still a stalemate?

no

Why not?

Although Black cannot move his King, he can move his Rook.

∞

But there is still a way that White can force a draw. This is called PERPETUAL CHECK. The unaided Queen cannot checkmate the Black King, but she can go on checking him endlessly.

Suppose that it is White's move. He moves Q-KR6 ch. What is Black's only possible move? ..._____

...K-KN1

∞

What move will White make to check him again? _____

Q-KN6 ch

∞

Why not Q-KN5 ch?

The King could escape via KB2.

∞

—185—

Write all possible capturing moves which the Bishop can make.

BxP, BxN, BxR

—186—

Place a White Bishop on K3; place a Black Rook on KB5, and a Black Knight on KN4.

Is the following move possible: BxN?

no
(The Bishop cannot jump over the Rook to capture the Knight.)

—187—

Place a White Knight on Q1 and a Black Rook on K6. Write a possible capturing move. _____

NxR
(The Knight moves one square straight forward and then one square diagonally to the right and captures the Rook.)

—188—

It is White's move. Write all the possible capturing moves.

NxB, NxR, NxQ

—412—

Place the Black King on K1, the Black Queen on K2, and a Black Rook on Q2; place a White Rook on QR8, and a White Knight on QB8.

What move will checkmate Black? _____

N-Q6 mate

∞

Why can't Black play ...QxN or ...RxN?

The King would still be in check from the Rook.

∞

Why can't Black play ...Q-Q1, interposing the Queen between the King and the White Rook?

The King would still be in check from the Knight.

∞

Why can't the King move to KB1 or Q1?

He would still be in check from the Rook.

∞

Why can't the King move to KB2?

He would still be in check from the Knight.

∞

The way in which White wins the game with this checkmate, when Black is far ahead in material, shows the great power of a _____ check.

double

—413—

What move will checkmate Black? _____

R-KB8 mate

—189—

Place a White Knight on Q2 and a Black Bishop on K6.

It is White's move.

Can the Knight capture the Bishop?

∞

If it were Black's move, would the following move be possible: ...BxN?

∞

Note that Black's moves are always preceded by three dots.

no

yes

—190—

Place a White Rook on Q1; place a Black Bishop on Q4, and a Black Knight on KN8. It is White's move.

Write all possible capturing moves. _____

RxB, RxN

—191—

Place a White Rook on QR1 and a Black Bishop on QB6.

It is White's move.

Is the following move possible: RxB?

∞

If it were Black's move, would the following move be possible: ...BxR?

∞

A move made by _____ has three dots in front of it.

∞

If a move is not preceded by three dots, you will know that it is made by _____.

no

yes

Black

White

—410—

Place the Black King on KR1, and a Black Bishop on KB1; place the White Queen on Q4, and a White Knight on K5.

White moves N-KN6 dbl ch. Can Black interpose the Bishop?

∞

Why not?

∞

Black has only two two possible moves, ..._____ or ..._____.

no	
The King would still be in check from the Knight.	
...K-KN1, ...K-KR2	

—411—

A double check often turns out to be a good way to checkmate your opponent. Place the Black King on KR1, and a Black Pawn on KR2; place a White Rook on KB6, and a White Bishop on K5. It is White's move. How can he checkmate Black with a double check? _____

∞

The King is in check from the _____ and the _____.

∞

If he moves to KN1, he is still in check from the _____.

∞

If he moves to KN2, he is still in check from the _____.

R-KB8 mate
Rook, Bishop
Rook
Bishop

—192—

Is the following move possible: RxQ?

no
(The Rook cannot jump over the Bishop to capture the Queen.)

∞

What capturing move is possible? _____

RxB

—193—

We have now practiced capturing with all chessmen except the Pawn.

All chessmen except the _____ capture the same way that they move.

Pawn

—194—

The Pawn's normal move is one square straight _____, but it captures by moving one square diagonally forward to the right or left.

forward

—195—

The x's show the two squares on which the White Pawn could make captures.

A Pawn captures _____.

diagonally

—407—

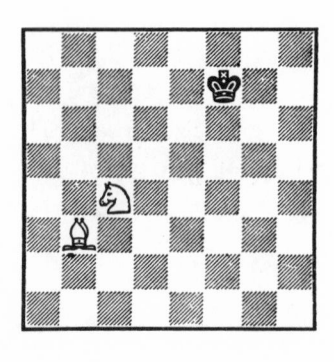

What are the two moves which will place the Black King in double check?

_____

_____

N-QN6 dbl ch,

N-QB7 dbl ch

—408—

Place the Black King on Q2; place a White Rook on Q1, and a White Bishop on Q3. What are the two moves which will place the Black King in double check?

_____

_____

B-QN5 dbl ch,

B-KB5 dbl ch

—409—

What are the two moves which will place the Black King in double check?

_____

_____

N-Q6 dbl ch,

N-K5 dbl ch

—196—

Can the White Pawn capture the Black Rook?

yes

—197—

Place a White Pawn on QN3. Place a Black Knight on QR5, and a Black Rook on QB5.

Write any possible capturing moves. _____

PxN, PxR

—198—

Place a White Pawn on K3, and a Black Rook on K5. Can the Pawn capture the Rook?

no
(The Pawn captures only diagonally.)

∞

Can the Pawn move to K4?

no
(The square is already occupied by the Rook, which the Pawn can- not capture.)

If he moves R-K5 ch, for example, he will win the Black
_____ if Black does not _____ the
Bishop between his King and the White Bishop by moving
…_____.

	Bishop
	interpose
	…B-QB3

∞

Place the pieces in the positions of the diagram.

_____

—405—

You will now learn a special case of a discovered check. This
is called DOUBLE CHECK (abbreviated "*dbl ch*").

If White moves R-QN5 dbl ch, Black's King is in check from
both the Bishop and the Rook. Why can't Black interpose his
Bishop between his King and the White Bishop?

He would still be in
check from the Rook.

∞

Why can't Black play …BxR to remove the checking Rook?

He would still be in
check from the Bishop.

∞

A chessplayer can escape from a double check only by
—*interposition/moving his King out of check/capturing a
checking piece.*

moving his King out
of check.

_____

—406—

Place the Black King on KR1; place a White Rook on K5,
and a White Bishop on QN2. In what two ways can White
place the Black King in double check?

_____, _____

R-K8 dbl ch,
R-KR5 dbl ch

—199—

List all possible capturing moves of the White Queen.

_____

QxR, QxP

_____

∞

The Queen cannot capture the White Bishop because he is one of her own men. She can capture only Black pieces.

Why can't she capture the Black Knight?

She can't jump over the White Bishop.

_____

—200—

List all possible capturing moves of the White Knight.

_____

NxB, NxQ, NxR

_____

—201—

List the possible capturing moves of the Pawn. _____

PxR, PxN

∞

_____

It cannot capture the Bishop because a Pawn captures only _____.

diagonally

White	Black	Position after 10...QxB

10.   B-QN5!!

This sacrifice wins the Black Queen.

                              10.   QxB

Check with diagram.

∞

What move now wins the Black Queen?

11.   _____   NxQBP ch

∞

This is called a Knight _____.   fork

∞

Black resigns -- he concedes defeat.

Remove all chessmen from the board.

—404—

If White moves his Rook, the re-   discovered
sult will be a _____
check from the White Bishop.

∞

—202—

When a White piece is in a position to capture a Black piece, we say that the White piece is ATTACKING the Black piece. Place a White Bishop on KB1, and a Black Rook on QB5.

Is the White Bishop attacking the Black Rook?

yes

∞

Is the Black Rook attacking the White Bishop?

no

—203—

How many pieces is the White Knight attacking?

three
(The Rook, Bishop, and Queen.)

∞

If the Black Knight were on KN3 instead of on KR3, how many pieces would the White Knight be attacking?

four
(He would then be attacking the Black Knight, in addition to the other Black pieces.)

—204—

Place the White Queen on QB4, and a Black Rook on K3. When the pieces are in this position, we say that the White Queen is _____ the Black Rook.

attacking

	White		Black
		5.	Q-K2?

This move is bad because it lets White's Knight attack the Queen.

Position after 8. B-KB4

6.	N-Q5!	6.	Q-Q3
7.	PxB	7.	QxP
8.	B-KB4		

Check with the diagram.

∞

What is White's threat? _____

BxN

∞

If Black moved the Knight away, how would White fork the Black King and the Queen Rook? _____

NxQBP ch

∞

Why does Black now move

in order to protect the threatened Knight

8. P-Q3

∞

9. P-QN4!

What is the only move which will save the Black Queen?

9. _____

...Q-QB3
(All other possible squares are attacked by White pieces.)

∞

—205—

In this position, the White Knight is _____ the Black King.

attacking

∞

When a player moves a piece to a square from which it attacks his opponent's King, he says *"check."* In this example the White Knight is said to be *"checking"* the Black King. The Black King is *"in check."*

Henceforth we shall always say that a piece is *"checking"* the opponent's King, instead of saying that it is attacking the King.

The only chessman that we are said to *"check"* instead of *"attack"* is the _____.

King

—206—

Place the White Queen on QR1 and the Black King on K4. In this position, the White Queen is _____ the Black King.

checking

∞

The Black King is in _____.

check

—207—

Place the Black King on KR1 and the White Queen on QN6. White moves the Queen from QN6 to KB6.

He says _____.

"check"

—403—

Set up the pieces in their starting positions, with the White chessmen nearest to you.

Make the following moves:

	White		Black
1.	P-K4	1.	P-K4
2.	N-KB3		

White is attacking Black's Pawn on _____.

K4

∞

What Knight move will defend this Pawn?

2. _____

...N-QB3

∞

Position after 4...NxN

| 3. | N-QB3 | 3. | B-QB4 |
| 4. | NxP | 4. | NxN |

Check with diagram.

∞

How can White regain his lost material?

5. _____

P-Q4

∞

This is an example of a Pawn _____.

fork

∞

—208—

The rules of Chess do not permit the King to move into check. If a player accidentally moves his King into check, he must take back the move and try another.

Place a White Rook on KR1 and the Black King on KN5. Can the Black King move to KR5?

no
(On KR5 the Black King would be in check from the White Rook. The King cannot move into check.)

—209—

Place a White Knight on KN1 and the Black King on K4. It is White's move. Where can the Knight move to check the Black King? _____

KB3

—210—

Place the Black King on KN1 and a White Bishop on KN2. Where can the Bishop move to check the Black King? _____

Q5

—211—

Place the Black King on QR3 and a White Pawn on QN4. If White advances his Pawn he must say _____.

"check"

∞

If White fails to notice that Black's King is in check, Black should point it out to him.

—212—

Where can the White Rook move to check the Black King? _____

K8

—400—

What move will win the Black Knight? _____

R-Q5 ch

—401—

The great power of the Queen makes numerous forks possible. She can fork enemy pieces on a diagonal, like the Bishop, or on a straight line like the Rook, or in positions where one piece is attacked on a diagonal and the other on a vertical or horizontal line.

Place the Black King on K1, and a Black Rook on KR4; place the White Queen on Q3. White has two moves which will win the Black Rook. What are they?_____, _____

Q-KN6 ch, Q-K2 ch

—402—

This diagram illustrates the enormous forking power of the Queen.

What move will win the Rook, Knight, or Bishop? _____

Q-QB6 ch

—213—

The record of a chess move consists of the abbreviation for the name of the chessman which makes the move, the abbreviation for "moves to," which is a short, straight line like the dash on a typewriter, and the abbreviation for the name of the square to which the chessman moves. Where Black's moves stand alone, they are generally preceded by _____ dots.

three

∞

Place a White Knight on KN1. Move the Knight to KB3. This move is written N-KB3.

Now place the same Knight on QN1, and then move it to QB3. Write the abbreviated version of this move. _____

N-QB3

—214—

Place the White Queen on Q5. Now move the Queen to KN5. Write this move in abbreviated form. _____

Q-KN5

—215—

Place a White Bishop on QB1. Move the Bishop to KB4. Write the abbreviated form of this move. _____

B-KB4

—216—

Write out in words the move which is abbreviated R-KN6. _____

Rook to King Knight six

---397---

Place the Black Knight on QN3, and a Black Rook on Q7; place a White Knight on Q6. It is White's move. What move does he make? _____

N-QB4 ch

∞

What must Black do?

He must move his King.

∞

Then White plays _____.

NxR

---398---

A Bishop can also fork two enemy pieces.

What move will fork the Black Rooks? _____

B-Q5

---399---

What move will win the Black Knight? _____

B-K6 ch

—217—

The abbreviation for *check* is "*ch.*" Place the Black King on K1, and the White Queen on QR1. If the Queen moves to K5 and checks the Black King, this move is written Q-K5 ch.

Now place the Queen back on QR1 and move her to K1.

Is the King in check?

∞

Write the abbreviated form of this move. _____

yes
Q-K1 ch

—218—

Place the Black King on QR1; place a White Knight on QB4. Write the abbreviation for the move which will put the Black King in check. _____

N-QN6 ch

—219—

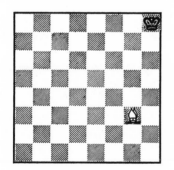

Write the move of the Bishop which checks the Black King. _____

B-K5 ch

—220—

A Chess player must always get his King out of check. Two ways of doing this are:

(1) move the King out of check,

(2) capture the piece which is checking the King.

Place the Black King on QR1; place the White Queen on QR7. The Black King is in _____.

check

∞

—395—

It is White's move. What move will he make? _____

N-Q4

∞

Does this fork the Black Rooks?

yes

∞

If Black moves one of the Rooks away, will White capture the other?

yes

—396—

Place the Black King on Q2, and the Black Queen on KN5; place a White Knight on QB4. It is White's move. What move will he make? _____

N-K5 ch

∞

Now Black must move his _____.

King

∞

And then White plays _____.

NxQ

Can Black move ...K-QN1?	no
∞	
Why not?	On QN1 the King is still in check from the White Queen.
∞	
Can Black move ...K-QN2?	no
∞	
Why not?	On QN2 the King is still in check.
∞	
Therefore Black's only possible move is ..._____.	...KxQ
∞	
A Black _____ which is written separately is preceded by three dots.	move

—221—

Place the Black King on KR1; place the White Queen on KR7.	
The Black King is ____ _____.	in check
∞	
What is Black's only possible move? ..._____	...KxQ
∞	
Why not ...K-KN1 or ...K-KN2?	He would still be in check from the Queen.

—392—

When two Black pieces are forked by a White Pawn, Black usually has the choice of which piece he wishes to move. But when one of the pieces is the King, Black has no choice because the King is ____ _____ and must be moved.

in check

—393—

Place the Black King on QN2, and a Black Rook on Q2; place White Pawns on QN5 and QB5. It is White's move. He plays P-QB6 ch. Black then moves his _____.

King

∞

And White plays _____.

PxR

—394—

Thus far you have practiced forks only with a Pawn, but a Knight can also fork opposing pieces.

Place the Black Queen on K4, and a Black Rook on KN4; place a White Knight on KN1. It is White's move. What move will he make? _____

N-KB3

∞

What will Black do then?

He will move the Queen.

∞

Why?

She is more valuable than the Rook.

∞

After Black moves the Queen, White will play _____.

NxR

—222—

Place the Black King on QR4; place the White Queen on QN5. The Black King is in check. What is his only possible move? ..._____

...KxQ

∞

Why couldn't he move to any of the adjacent squares?

He would still be in check from the Queen.

—223—

Place the Black King on QR1; place the White Queen on QR6. Is the Black King in check?

yes

∞

Can he capture the Queen?

no

∞

What is his only possible move? ..._____

...K-QN1

∞

Why couldn't he move to QR2 or QN2?

He would still be in check from the Queen.

—224—

Place the Black King on K1; place the White Queen on K6. Is the King in check?

yes

∞

What are his only possible moves? ..._____ ..._____

...K-Q1, ...K-KB1

∞

Why can't he move to any of the other adjacent squares?

He would still be in check from the Queen.

This opening in which White offers his KBP is called the KING'S GAMBIT.

2.   PxP

When Black captures the gambit Pawn, we say that he accepts the gambit, and the opening is then called the KING'S GAMBIT ACCEPTED.

3.   Q-KB3?

The question mark indicates that this is a bad move. White has brought his Queen out early and placed her on a spot where she blocks the development of his Knight to KB3.

3.   N-QB3

4.   N-K2?

Another bad move. On this square, the Knight blocks the development of the White King Bishop.

4.   B-QB4

5.   P-Q3   5.   P-KN4!

The exclamation point indicates that this is a good move. Black protects the Pawn which he has won and restricts White's play on the King side.

6.   P-KN3??

The double question mark indicates a very bad move.

6.   N-K4!

7.   ·Q-KN2

What move will now win the White Knight on K2?

7.   _____   ...P-KB6

∞

This is an example of a Pawn _____.   fork

∞

Remove all pieces from the board.

—225—

You have probably noticed that we have never shown the capture of a King. There was a good reason for this. When the King is placed in check and has no defense against the attack, he is said to be CHECKMATED. This is the end of the game. The Chess game ends when one player has _____ his opponent's King.

checkmated

∞

The player who has been checkmated has —won/lost— the game.

lost

—226—

This is an example of checkmate. The Black King is checked by the White Queen. He cannot move to any square where he will not be checked by the Queen, since the Queen covers all of the adjacent squares. He cannot capture the Queen because he would then be exposed to check from the Rook. That is, he would be moving into check.

The King can never move into _____.

check

∞

(In an actual game, the White King would also be present somewhere on the board. To save time in setting up the pieces in this frame and in many others to come, we have eliminated the White King when he does not take part in the play.)

White will then play _____.

PxB

∞

Black will move his Knight away from the attacking_____.

Pawn

—390—

Place the Black King on KB4, and a Black Knight on KR4; place White Pawns on KN3 and KR3. It is White's move. He plays _____.

P-KN4 ch

∞

Black must now move the _____.

King

∞

White's next move will be _____.

PxN

∞

Note that, as a result of capturing the Knight, White ends up with two _____ on the same file. These are called DOUBLED PAWNS.

Pawns

—391—

In the following game, White wins a piece with a Pawn fork. Set up the pieces in their starting positions, with the Black chessmen on your side of the board.

Make the following moves:

White	Black
1. P-K4	1. P-K4
2. P-KB4	

∞

—227—

This position is a _____,
because the Black King is in_____
and cannot move out of check.

checkmate
check

—228—

A King can never move to a square adjacent to the other King.
He cannot do this because he would be moving into _____.

check

∞

Consequently a King —*can/cannot*— check or checkmate
the other King.

cannot

∞

Can a King protect the piece which does the actual checkmating?

yes

—229—

Place the Black King on KB8; place the White Queen on
KB2. Is the Black King in check?

yes

∞

Is the position a checkmate?

no

∞

Why not?

Black can play ...KxQ

∞

Add a White Pawn on KR4. How can White win a Bishop or a Knight for a Pawn? _____

P-KN5

∞

If Black moves the Bishop away, White will play _____ .

PxN

∞

And if Black moves the Knight away, White will play _____ .

PxB

∞

Therefore Black plays ..._____ in order to get something for his Bishop.

...BxP

∞

Black has lost a Bishop for a Pawn. He will now move the _____ away from the attacking _____ .

Knight
Pawn

———

—389—

Place a Black Knight on QB4, and a Black Bishop on K4; place White Pawns on K3 and Q3. It is White's move. He will move _____ .

P-Q4

∞

He has _____ the Knight and the Bishop.

forked

∞

Black will probably play ..._____ .

...BxP

∞

Why?

in order to get something (a Pawn) for his lost Bishop

∞

Place a White Rook on KB3 behind the White Queen. Now is the position a checkmate?

yes

∞

Why can't Black play ...KxQ?

He would be moving into check from the White Rook.

∞

Remember that if the checking piece is placed on a square adjacent to the checked King, it must be protected by another piece. Otherwise, the King will simply _____ it.

capture

—230—

Place the Black King on KR8; place the White Queen on KN2, and a White Bishop on KB3.

This position is called _____.

checkmate

∞

Why can't Black play ...KxQ?

He would be moving into check from the Bishop.

—231—

The abbreviation for checkmate is MATE. Place the Black King on QB8; place the White King on Q3, and the White Queen on KR2. The White Queen moves to QB2 and checkmates the Black King. Write this move in abbreviated form. _____

Q-QB2 mate

This position of the diagram illustrates a FORK. This is a simultaneous attack on _____ enemy pieces.

two

∞

Let us now suppose that it is Black's move. He cannot avoid losing one of his pieces. He will move the _____ away and leave the _____ to be captured by the Pawn.

Rook
Knight

—387—

When a chessman attacks two enemy pieces simultaneously, this is called a _____.

fork

∞

Place one Black Rook on QN3, and the other Black Rook on Q3; place a White Pawn on QB4. It is White's move. How does he win a Rook? _____

P-QB5
(Black can move only one of the Rooks away on his next move. White will then capture the other one.)

—388—

If one of the pieces which a Pawn attacks can capture diagonally, then the Pawn must be protected by another piece. Otherwise, the opponent will simply capture the Pawn.

Place a Black Knight on KB3, and a Black Bishop on KR3; place a White Pawn on KN4. Will White win a piece if he plays P-KN5?

no

∞

Why not?

The Bishop will simply capture the Pawn.

∞

—383—

Place a Black Rook on Q5, and a Black Knight on KB7; place the White King on K3. It is White's move. What move should he make? _____

KxR

—384—

It is White's move. What move should he make? _____

PxR

—385—

Place a Black Bishop on K3, and a Black Knight on KN3; place a White Pawn on KB5. It is White's move. What move should he make? _____

PxB or PxN

∞

These moves are equally good since the Black pieces are of —*the same value/different values.*

the same value

—386—

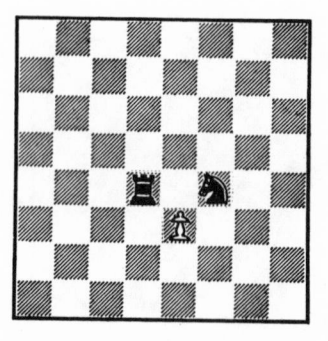

It is White's move. What move should he make? _____

PxR
(The Rook is more valuable than the Knight.)

The King can't move out of check. The White Rook now covers Black's _____, the only square which the Queen does not cover.

KR2

—235—

It is White's move. What move will checkmate Black?_____

∞

Why not Q-QR1 ch?

Q-QB8 mate

Black could move ...K-QN1 where he would be out of check.

—236—

Place the Black King on KR8; place a White Rook on QR2, and the White Queen on K6. It is White's move. What move will checkmate Black? _____

∞

Why can't Black move ...K-KR7?

∞

If White had moved Q-KR3, would the Black King be in check?

∞

Would it be a checkmate?

∞

Why not?

Q-K1 mate

He would be in check from the Rook.

yes

no

The King could move to KN8 where he would be out of check.

—379—

Place a Black Rook on QB3, a Black Bishop on K3, and a Black Knight on KN7; place the White Queen on K4. It is White's move. What move should he make? _____

QxR

—380—

It is White's move. What move should he make? _____

PxQ

—381—

Place a Black Rook on QR3, and a Black Knight on QB3; place a White Pawn on QN5. It is White's move. What move should he make? _____

PxR

—382—

It is White's move. What move should he make? _____

KxN
(The King could have captured the Pawn, but the Knight is more valuable than the Pawn.)

—237—

What move will checkmate
Black? _____

Q-QR8 mate

∞

Q-QB4 ch fails to checkmate Black because he can move
either ..._____ or ..._____.

...K-QR4, ...K-QR6

—238—

Thus far only the Queen has moved to checkmate the Black
King. Other pieces may also be used. Here is an example
in which the King is checkmated by a Rook.

What move will checkmate
Black? _____

R-KR6 mate

—239—

Place the Black King on K1; place the White Queen on
QN7 and the White Rook on KR1. What move will checkmate Black? _____

R-KR8 mate

∞

Why not BxN?

The Rook is more valuable than the Knight.

—376—

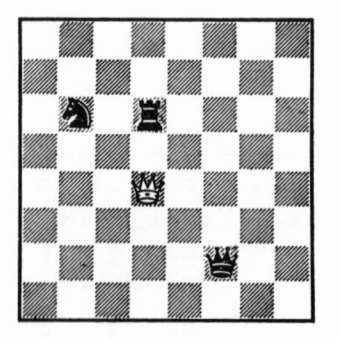

It is White's move. What move should he make? _____

QxQ
(The Queen is more valuable than the Rook or the Knight.)

—377—

Place a Black Knight on QB3, a Black Bishop on KN3, and a Black Rook on KR8; place a White Bishop on K4. It is White's move. What move should he make? _____

BxR
(The Rook is more valuable than either the Knight or the Bishop.)

—378—

It is White's move. What move should he make? _____

8

If the Queen weren't there, what move should he have made? _____

NxQ

NxR

This position is a checkmate because the Black King is
____ _____ and cannot move out of _____

| in check |
| check |

∞

The King cannot escape from the Rook by moving to K2, for
example, because this square is covered by the _____.

Queen

—240—

White can also checkmate Black with a Queen and a Bishop.

What move of the Queen will
checkmate Black? _____

Q-QN7 mate

∞

Is Q-QR7 a checkmate?

no

∞

Why not?

Black simply plays
...KxQ.

—241—

Place the Black King on KR1; place a White Bishop on KN8,
and the White Queen on QN1. What move will checkmate
Black? _____

Q-KR7 mate

∞

This position is a checkmate because the Black King is in
check from the _____.

Queen

∞

Black cannot move out of check, and he cannot capture the
Queen because she is protected by the _____.

Bishop

∞

—372—

Place the Black Rook on QN4, and the Black Queen on Q4; place a White Knight on QB3. It is White's move. What move should he make? _____

∞

Why not NxR?

NxQ

The Queen is more valuable than the Rook.

—373—

It is White's move. What move should he make? _____

BxQ

—374—

Place a Black Rook on QB6, and a Black Bishop on K2. Place a White Knight on Q5. It is White's move. What move should he make? _____

∞

Why not NxB?

NxR

The Rook is more valuable than the Bishop.

—375—

Place a Black Rook on QR2, and a Black Knight on KR1. Place a White Bishop on Q4. It is White's move. What move should he make? _____

∞

BxR

Black cannot capture the _____ because it is protected by the Queen.

Bishop

—242—

Place the Black King on QR8; place a White Bishop on QB1, and the White Queen on KR2. What move will checkmate Black? _____

∞

Q-QN2 mate

Why can't Black play ...KxQ?

He would be moving into check from the Bishop.

—243—

Place the Black King on QR5; place a White Bishop on QB5, and the White Queen on QN1. What move will checkmate Black? _____

∞

Q-QN4 mate

This position is a checkmate for the following reasons:

(a) The Black King is in check from the White _____.

Queen

∞

(b) He cannot capture the Queen because he would then be in check from the White _____.

Bishop

∞

(c) He can't move to any of the adjacent squares because they are all covered by the _____.

Queen

Since the King is never captured, we cannot compare his value to that of the other pieces. Although the _____ is a relatively weak piece, it is obvious that he cannot be removed from the chessboard during a game.

King

—367—

As you have probably guessed, the _____ is the most powerful piece on the chessboard.

Queen

—368—

The _____ is less powerful than the Queen, but more powerful than the Knight or the Bishop.

Rook

—369—

The _____ and the Bishop are of equal value.

Knight

—370—

The least valuable chessmen are the _____.

Pawns

—371—

In a game of Chess, you seek to capture your opponent's most valuable pieces, while keeping him from capturing your chessmen. You will try to get his most powerful pieces off the board as fast as possible if you can do so without loss to yourself. Whenever there is a choice between capturing one or another of his pieces, you will, of course, capture the more powerful piece.

The most important of the opposing pieces for you to capture is the _____.

Queen

—244—

What move will checkmate Black? _____

Q-KN3 mate

—245—

Thus far, when we have used a Queen and a Bishop, it has always been the Queen which has checkmated the Black King. Aided by the Queen, a Bishop can also checkmate the opposing King.

Place the Black King on QR8; place the White Queen on QN3, and a White Bishop on K1. What move will checkmate Black? _____

B-QB3 mate

∞

Why can't Black move ...K-QN8?

He would be moving into check from the Queen.

—246—

Place the Black King on KR1; place the White Queen on KB7, and a White Bishop on KN1. What move will checkmate Black? _____

B-Q4 mate

∞

Why can't Black move ...K-KR2?

He would be moving into check from the Queen.

Note that if White had played N-KB3 on the third move, the _____ would have been in a position to capture the Black Queen if she moved to KR5.

∞

Replace the chessmen in their starting positions.

	Knight

—365—

Make the following moves:

	White		Black
1.	P-K4	1.	P-K4
2.	B-QB4	2.	B-QB4
3.	Q-KB3		

What is White's threat? _____

QxKBP mate

∞

Give six moves which will stop this threat.

···_____, ···_____,
···_____, ···_____,
···_____, ···_____.

...N-KB3, ...Q-K2,
...Q-KB3, ...P-KB3,
...N-KR3, ...K-K2

∞

Remove all chessmen from the board.

—366—

When a chess player captures more pieces, or more valuable pieces, than he loses, we say that he is ahead in material. The superiority of his forces often enables him to win the game by forcing checkmate.

In order to know which of your opponent's pieces you should capture when you're given a choice, you must know the relative value of the chessmen.

∞

—247—

What move will checkmate
Black? _____

B-Q5 mate

—248—

This time it is a Knight which aids the White Queen. After
a Knight moves one square backward, it then moves one
square _____ to the left or the right.

diagonally

∞

Place the Black King on Q8; place a White Knight on K4,
and the White Queen on KR2. What move will checkmate
Black? _____

Q-Q2 mate

∞

This position is a checkmate for the following reasons:

(a) The Black King is checked by the White
     —Queen/Knight.

Queen

∞

(b) He cannot capture the White Queen because he would
     then be —captured by/in check from— the White Knight.

in check from

∞

(c) He cannot move to any of the adjacent squares because
     they are all covered by the _____ .

Queen

This is the third shortest way of ending a Chess game. It is called SCHOLAR'S MATE, and has been used against beginners for centuries. Black's opening technique was good, but he forgot to protect his _____.

King

∞

Replace all the chessmen in their starting positions.

—364—

White opens with P-K4. Black also moves ..._____.

...P-K4

∞

White's second move is N-QB3. Black then moves ...B-QB4.

White moves B-QB4; Black's third move ...Q-KR5. What is Black's threat? ..._____

...QxKBP mate

∞

Find five moves for White which will prevent this check-mate. _____, _____, _____, _____, _____

N-KR3, P-KN3, Q-K2, Q-KB3, K-K2

∞

Why not P-Q4?

Black would play ...BxP and White would still be facing the same threat of mate.

∞

Would N-KB3 help White?

no

∞

Why not?

Black would play ...QxKBP mate.

∞

—249—

Place the Black King on QR8; place a White Knight on QB4, and the White Queen on K2. What move will checkmate Black? _____

Q-QN2 mate

∞

Why not Q-Q1 ch?

Black would move ...K-QR7 where he would be out of check.

—250—

What move will checkmate Black? _____

Q-QB7 mate

—251—

What move will checkmate Black? _____

Q-KN6 mate

—363—

Set up the pieces in their starting positions with the Black chessmen on your side of the board. The Black King is on the _____ side of the Black Queen.

left

∞

Can you suggest a good opening move for White? _____

P-K4
(P-Q4 is also a strong opening move.)

∞

Make the following moves:

White		Black	
1.	P-K4	1.	P-K4
2.	B-QB4	2.	B-QB4
3.	Q-KR5	3.	N-QB3

Check with the diagram.

∞

It is White's fourth move.

What move will checkmate Black? _____

QxKBP mate

∞

This is a checkmate because the Black _____ is in check from the White _____.

King
Queen

∞

Why can't Black capture the Queen?

He would be moving into check from the White Bishop.

∞

Why can't the Black King move to KB1 or to K2?

He would still be in check from the Queen.

∞

—252—

The _____ is the only piece which can jump over other chessmen, whether Black or White.

Knight

∞

Aided by the Queen, a Knight can also checkmate the opposing King. Place the Black King on QR8; place the White Queen on QB2, and a White Knight on Q2. What move of the Knight will checkmate Black? _____

N-QN3 mate

∞

Why not N-QN1?

The Black King would not be in check.

—253—

Place the Black King on KR1; place the White Queen on KB7, and the White Knight on K7. What move of the Knight will checkmate Black? _____

N-KN6 mate

∞

This is a checkmate for the following reasons:

(a) The Black King is in check from the White _____.

Knight

∞

(b) He cannot move to any of the three adjacent squares because he would then be in check from the White _____.

Queen

∞

Now move the Knight back to K7. What move of the Queen will checkmate Black? _____

Q-KN8 mate

∞

Why can't Black play ...KxQ?

He would be moving into check from the Knight.

—361—

Place the Black King on QN2, and a Black Bishop on QR5; place a White Bishop on KN2, and a White Rook on KB3. White moves R-QR3 dis ch.

What is the only move which will save the Black Bishop from capture by the White Rook? ..._____

...B-QB3
(Black gets his King out of check and his Bishop out of danger in one move by interposing his Bishop between the King and the White Bishop which is checking him.)

—362—

The Pawns are named for the pieces in front of which they stand. The Pawn in front of the King is called the _____ Pawn.

∞

The Pawn in front of the Queen Knight is called the _____ _____ _____.

∞

The abbreviation for this is _____.

∞

KRP is the abbreviation for _____ _____ _____.

∞

We shall use these names to avoid ambiguity when capturing Pawns.

King
(abbreviated KP)

Queen Knight Pawn

QNP

King Rook Pawn

—254—

Place the Black King on QR1; place the White Queen on QN6, and a White Knight on Q5. What move will checkmate Black? _____

∞

Why not Q-QR6 ch?

N-QB7 mate

Black can move ...K-QN1 where he is out of check.

—255—

What move will checkmate Black? _____

∞

Why not Q-KB2?

Q-KN1 mate

The Black King would not be in check.

—256—

Here is a different pattern of checkmate, with a Queen and a Bishop.

Place the Black King on KR8; place the White Queen on QB4, and a White Bishop on KB4. What move will checkmate Black? _____

∞

Why not Q-QB1 ch?

∞

Why not Q-K4 ch?

Q-KB1 mate

The King can move to KN7 where he is out of check.

The King can move to KN8 where he is out of check.

Black has interposed his Rook between the King and the Queen which was checking him. White can, of course, still play QxR ch, but Black will then play _____ and White will not have won a Rook, but will have exchanged it for a Queen -- a poor bargain, as we shall see shortly.

...KxQ

—359—

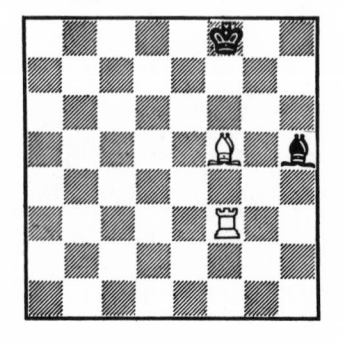

White moves B-KN4 dis ch. If Black moves his King out of check, White's Bishop will then capture the Black Bishop. What is the only move which will save the Bishop? _____

...B-KB2
(Black has interposed the Bishop between the Rook and the King. His King is now out of check.)

—360—

Place the Black King on KN2, and a Black Knight on Q2; place the White Queen on QB3, and a White Pawn on K5.

White plays P-K6 dis ch. What is the only move which will save the Black Knight from being captured? _____

...N-KB3
(This was the only way in which Black could get his King out of check and save the Knight from the attacking Pawn in one move.)

Why not ...N-K4?

On K4 the Knight is not protected by the King. White will reply QxN ch.

—257—

Place the Black King on KR1; place the White Queen on QR3, and a White Bishop on K4. What move will checkmate Black? _____

Q-KB8 mate

—258—

What move will checkmate Black? _____

Q-QB8 mate

—259—

Place the Black King on QR1; place a White Knight on QB8, and the White Queen on K7. What move will checkmate Black? _____

∞

Why can't Black play ...KxQ?

Q-QR7 mate

He would be moving into check from the Knight.

—260—

What move will checkmate Black? _____

∞

Why not Q-KB1 ch?

Q-Q2 mate

Black can move ...K-QB7 where he is out of check.

The Black King moves; then White plays _____.	PxB

—357—

As you have already learned, there are three possible ways for a Chess player to get his King out of check:

(1) He can simply _____ out of check.	move
∞	
(2) He can _____ the checking piece.	capture
∞	
(3) He can _____ one of his pieces between the King and the checking piece.	interpose
∞	
This third possibility is often useful in saving a piece which has been attacked through a —*smothered mate/discovered check*.	discovered check
∞	
Can the attacked piece sometimes both get the King out of check and be protected by the King?	yes

---

—358—

Place the Black King on KB1, and a Black Rook on QB2; place the White Queen on KB1, and a White Bishop on KB2. White moves B-QN6 dis ch.

Now Black's King is in check from the White Queen, and his Rook is attacked by the White Bishop. What is the only move which will get the King out of check and save the Black Rook from being captured by the Bishop? ..._____	...,R-KB2

∞

—261—

Place the Black King on QR1; place a White Pawn on QR7, and the White Queen on QN5. What move will checkmate Black? _____

∞

With the pieces in this checkmate position, state why Black can't make any of the following moves:

...KxP

∞

...KxQ

∞

...K-QN2

Q-QN8 mate

_____

He would be moving into check from the Queen.

_____

He would be moving into check from the Pawn.

_____

He would be moving into check from the Queen.

_____

—262—

What move will checkmate Black? _____

Q-KN7 mate

_____

—263—

Place the Black King on Q1; place a White Pawn on QB6, and the White Queen on KR7. What move will checkmate Black? _____

∞

Q-Q7 mate

—354—

It is White's move.

What move will win the Black Rook? _____

N-QN4 dis ch

∞

The Black King moves out of check; then White plays _____.

NxR

—355—

Place the Black King on QB2, and a Black Bishop on KB2; place a White Bishop on KN3, and a White Pawn on K5.

It is White's move.

What move will win the Black Bishop? _____

P-K6 dis ch

∞

The Black King is in check from the White —*Pawn/Bishop.*

Bishop

∞

He must move out of check. Then White will play _____.

PxB

—356—

It is White's move.

How does he win the Black Bishop? _____

P-Q5 dis ch

∞

Why not P-QB7 ch?

Black would move
...K-QB1 or ...K-K1.

—264—

What move will checkmate
Black? _____

Q-QN7 mate

∞

Why not P-QR7?

The Black King would
not be in check.

—265—

What move will checkmate
Black? _____

Q-KB7 mate

—266—

If a Pawn is aided only by the Queen, there is still a way for
the Pawn to checkmate the opponent's King. You have
already learned that when a Pawn reaches the _____
rank it can be replaced by any other piece of its own color
(except a King).

eighth

∞

The Pawn is usually replaced by a _____. The symbol
for the queening of a Pawn is /Q. Thus Pawn to King 8
(queens) is abbreviated P-K8/Q.

Queen

—351—

Place the Black King on QB1, and a Black Bishop on KN5. Place a White Knight on QB6, and a White Rook on QB3.

It is White's move.

What move will win the Black Bishop? _____

∞

The King must move out of check from the Rook. White will then play _____.

N-K5 dis ch

_____

NxB

—352—

It is White's move.

What move will win the Black Knight? _____

∞

The Black King is in check from the Bishop and must move out of check. White will then play _____.

R-KN4 dis ch

_____

RxN

—353—

Place the Black King on K2, and a Black Knight on QR5; place a White Knight on K6, and the White Queen on K1.

It is White's move.

How does he win the Black Knight? _____

∞

The Black King is in check from the White Queen. He must move out of check. White will then play _____.

N-QB5 dis ch

_____

NxN

—267—

In the game of Chess, it is possible to have two or even three or more Queens of the same color on the board at the same time. Place the Black King on KB1; place a White Pawn on Q7, and the White Queen on KR7. What move will checkmate Black? _____

∞

If you were playing in a tournament or a match, you would be provided with another Queen. Extra Queens are not included in Chess sets because you would use them rarely. For the present, simply treat your Pawn which has queened as a Queen. To avoid confusion, Chess players often use an inverted Rook as a new _____.

P-Q8/Q mate
(or P-Q8/R mate)

Queen

—268—

What move will checkmate Black? _____

P-Q8/Q mate
(or P-Q8/R mate)

—269—

Place the Black King on KR1; place a White Pawn on KB7, and the White Queen on KN6. White has four possible ways of checkmating Black. What are they?

_____   _____

_____   _____

P-KB8/Q mate,
Q-KN8 mate,
Q-KR6 mate,
P-KB8/R mate

—349—

Place the Black King on QR3, and a Black Rook on QR7;
place a White Bishop on QB6, and a White Rook on
Q6. It is White's move. What move will win the Black
Rook? _____

B-Q5 dis ch

∞

The Black King has to move out of _____, and White's
next move is _____.

check
BxR

—350—

It is White's move.

What move will win the Black
Rook? _____

N-K7 dis ch

∞

The Black King is in check from the White _____.

Queen

∞

What must Black do?

He must move out of
check.

∞

White will then play _____.

NxR

—270—

Place the Black King on QR1; place a White Pawn on QN6, and the White Queen on Q7. White has two possible ways of checkmating Black. What are they?

_____   _____

Q-QR7 mate,
Q-QB8 mate

_____

—271—

What move will checkmate Black? _____

Q-KR6 mate

∞

_____

Why not P-KB8/Q ch?

Black can still move ...K-KR2.

_____

—272—

Two Rooks can force checkmate in much the same way that the Queen and a Rook did.

Place the Black King on KR1; place a White Rook on Q7, and the other White Rook on QR5. What move will checkmate Black? _____

R(QR5)-QR8 mate

—347—

What is the Bishop's only possible move? _____

BxR dis ch

∞

Black has _____ possible moves.

two

∞

What are they? ..._____, ..._____

...KxB, ...K-QN2

—348—

It is usually easier to checkmate your opponent when you have captured most of his pieces. A discovered check often leads to the capture of a piece.

Place the Black King on KN1, and a Black Rook on QB1. Place a White Bishop on KN6, and a White Rook on KN4. White plays B-KB5 dis ch.

The King is in check from the White Rook. He has to move out of check. This means that Black has no chance to move his Rook which is attacked by the Bishop; so White will play _____ and will gain a Rook.

BxR

∞

If, instead of moving B-KB5 dis ch, White had moved B-KR5 dis ch, would he have won the Black Rook?

no

∞

Why not?

On KR5, the Bishop is not attacking the Rook.

—273—

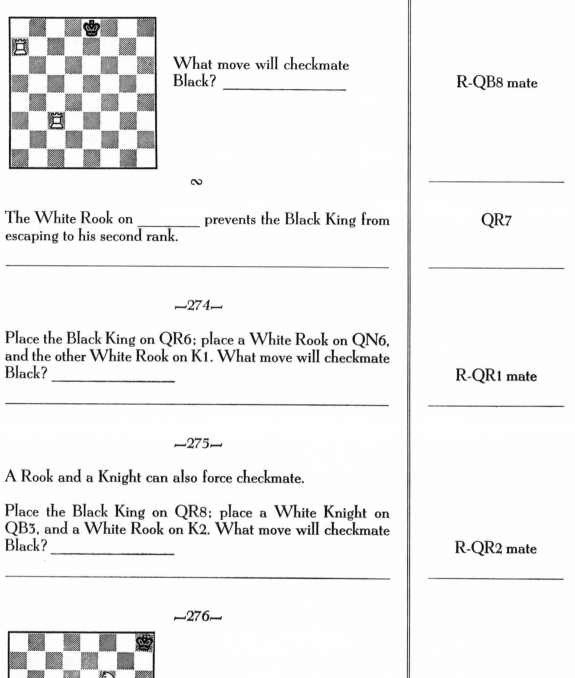

What move will checkmate Black? _____

R-QB8 mate

∞

The White Rook on _____ prevents the Black King from escaping to his second rank.

QR7

—274—

Place the Black King on QR6; place a White Rook on QN6, and the other White Rook on K1. What move will checkmate Black? _____

R-QR1 mate

—275—

A Rook and a Knight can also force checkmate.

Place the Black King on QR8; place a White Knight on QB3, and a White Rook on K2. What move will checkmate Black? _____

R-QR2 mate

—276—

What move will checkmate Black? _____

R-KN8 mate

—343—

How does White place the Black King in check from his Rook?

∞

This is called a _____ check.

With any move of the Knight.

discovered

—344—

White can place the Black King in check from his Queen by moving either the Queen or the Rook.

If he places the Black King in check from the White Queen by moving the _____, this is called a discovered check.

Rook

—345—

Place the Black King on Q1; place a White Bishop on QR5, and a White Pawn on QN6. What is the only move which will place the Black King in check? _____

P-QN7 dis ch

—346—

Sometimes it is possible to give discovered check by means of a capture.

Place the Black King on KN1, and a Black Pawn on KB3. Place a White Pawn on KN5, and a White Rook on KN4.

What is the only move which will place the Black King in check? _____

PxP dis ch

—277—

Place the Black King on QR8; place a White Bishop on QB1, and a White Knight on QB3. Is the Black King in check?

no

_____

∞

Can the King move to any square where he is not in check?

no

_____

It is Black's move. As matters stand, he is not in check, but he cannot move without moving _____ _____.
This position is called STALEMATE.

into check

_____

∞

STALEMATE and CHECKMATE are alike in that in both cases a player is limited to moves that would place his _____ in _____.

King
check

_____

∞

There is one big difference between stalemate and checkmate. In checkmate, the King is in check to begin with, whereas in _____ the King is not in check.

stalemate

_____

∞

There is also a great difference in the result of the game. You win when you _____ your opponent; when you stalemate your opponent, the game is a draw.

checkmate

—340—

When a piece attacks the hostile King, the King is said to be ____ _____ .

∞

There is another way to place the _____ in check. White can move a piece which has been blocking another of his own chessmen from checking the Black King. This is called DIS-COVERED CHECK, which is abbreviated *"dis ch."*

—341—

Place the Black King on K1; place a White Rook on K4, and a White Bishop on K5. What piece must White move in order to place the Black King in check?

∞

Any move of the Bishop places the Black King in check from the White —*Bishop/Rook.*

∞

This is called —*an interposition/a discovered check.*

—342—

Place the Black King on QB1; place a White Bishop on KN4, and a White Rook on K6. What piece must White move to place Black in check?

∞

Any move of the Rook places the Black King in check from the White _____ .

---

in check

King

the White Bishop

Rook

a discovered check

the Rook

Bishop

—278—

Place the Black King on KR1; place a White Bishop on KB8, and a White Knight on KB6. It is Black's move.

Is Black's King in check?

no

∞

Does Black's King have any move that will not bring him into check?

no

∞

Is this position a stalemate?

yes

∞

Why is it a stalemate?

The King is not in check, but he cannot move without moving into check.

∞

Is this position a checkmate?

no

∞

Why isn't it a checkmate?

Because in checkmate the King must be in check.

—339—

Place the Black King on QR1, and the White Queen on QB7. It is Black's move. This position is called a _____ .

∞

Is the King in check?

∞

Can he move without placing himself in check?

∞

Therefore he has —*won/lost/drawn*— the game.

∞

Add a White Bishop on KB2. If it is Black's move, the position is a _____ and the game is a _____ .

∞

If it is White's move, he has two possible ways to checkmate Black. What are they?

_____ , _____

∞

Why not B-QR7

∞

If the White Queen checks the Black King on either QN7 or QN8, the King simply _____ the Queen.

∞

If the Queen checks him on Q8, the King moves to _____ where he is out of check.

---

stalemate

no

no

drawn

stalemate
draw

Q-QR7 mate,
Q-QB8 mate

The Black King would
not be in check.

captures

QN2

—279—

It is Black's move. This position is a _____.

∞

Why isn't it a checkmate?

stalemate

The Black King is not in check.

—280—

Place the Black King on QN1; place a White Pawn on QB7, and the White King on QN6.

The Black King is ____ _____.

∞

He has two possible squares to which he may move. If he moves to QR1, he will lose the game because the White Pawn will become a _____, giving checkmate.

∞

If he moves to QB1 the game will be a _____, because the White King must either move to QB6 and _____ Black, or move away and let him capture the Pawn.

in check

Queen (or Rook)

draw
stalemate

—281—

Place the Black King on K1; place a White Pawn on K7, and the White King on KB5. It is White's move. What move should he avoid because it will stalemate Black? _____

∞

What move will protect the Pawn without stalemating Black? _____

∞

K-K6

K-KB6

—338—

On the basis of your experience in the last game, could you suggest a good opening move for White? _____

∞

P-K4

_____

Black's first move is ...P-KN4.

White then moves P-Q4 and Black replies ...P-KB3. Check with the diagram.

∞

_____

What move will now checkmate Black? _____

Q-KR5 mate

∞

_____

This game was a _____ Mate in reverse, in which White checkmates Black on his third move.

Fool's

∞

_____

Note that if Black had played P-KB4 instead of P-KB3, it would still be a _____.

checkmate

∞

_____

Note also that after playing P-K4, White could have played N-QB3, B-QB4, P-Q3, or any other second move which did not block the Queen's diagonal to the checkmating position on _____.

KR5

∞

Remove all pieces from the board.

What is Black's only possible move? ..._____

...K-Q2

∞

White will then move _____ to protect the Pawn and assure its queening.

K-KB7

∞

And White will win the game because the Black King must move away and can no longer prevent the White Pawn from becoming a Queen. A King and _____ can force a checkmate.

Queen

—282—

Here is another example where winning the game depends on whose move it is.

If it is White's move, he wins by moving _____.

Q-QN2 mate

∞

But if it is Black's move, the game is a _____, because the Black King is _____.

draw
stalemated

Can White capture the Queen?	no
∞	
Can he interpose any of his pieces?	no
∞	
Can he move his King out of check?	no
∞	
He would still be in check on KB2, the only square to which he could move. Therefore the position is a _____.	checkmate
∞	
This checkmate in two moves is the shortest possible Chess game. It has been known for many years as FOOL'S MATE. It illustrates the dangers which beset a beginner who knows how to move his individual chessmen, but has no idea of certain general principles of Chess. Let us make a start toward formulating one of these rules by saying that a player should not begin by moving his King Bishop Pawn and his _____ _____ Pawn.	King Knight
∞	
On the basis of Black's success, we may conclude that _____ is a strong first move.	P-K4
∞	
It opens up diagonals for both the _____ and the King _____.	Queen Bishop
∞	
Replace the pieces in their starting positions.	

—283—

If it is White's move, he wins the game by moving _____.

∞

But if it is Black's move, the King is _____.

R-KR4 mate

stalemated

—284—

If it is Black's move, the position is a _____.

∞

If it is White's move, he checkmates Black by moving _____.

stalemate

Q-KR6 mate

—285—

It is Black's move. This position is a _____.

∞

Why can't the Black King move?

stalemate

He would be moving into check.

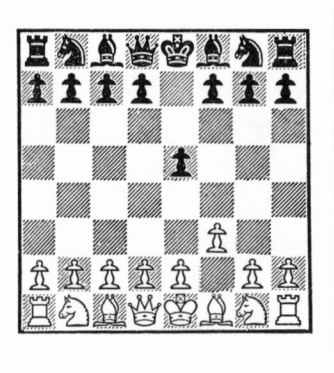

White's first move is P-KB3. Black's first move is ...P-K4. Check with the diagram.

∞

Whose move is it?   White's

∞

White plays P-KN4. Make this move and check with the diagram.

∞

Black's second move is ...Q-KR5. Make this move and check with the diagram.

∞

White's King is in check. As you know, there are three possible ways to get out of check. White must be able either to _____ the Queen, or to _____ one of his men between his King and the checking Queen, or to _____ his King out of check.

capture
interpose
move

∞

—286—

Place the Black King on KR1; place White Pawns on KB6, KN6, and KR6. What is the only Pawn move which White can make without stalemating Black? _____

P-KN7 ch

∞

Why not P-KR7?

The Black King could not move, because he would be moving into check.

∞

Is this also true for the move P-KB7?

yes

—287—

Thus far we have practiced checkmates when the Black King was the only Black piece remaining on the board. When the King is accompanied by other Black chessmen, checkmates are sometimes harder and sometimes easier.

Place a Black Pawn on QR2, and the Black King on QR1; place the White Queen on QB1. What move will check-mate Black? _____

Q-QB8 mate

∞

This checkmate is made possible because the Black _____ blocks the escape of the Black _____.

Pawn
King

—288—

Again place the Black King on QR1 and a Black Pawn on QR2, but this time place a White Rook on QB1. Now it is the Rook, instead of the Queen, which moves to QB8 and checks the Black King. Is this a checkmate?

no

∞

—336—

White plays Q-Q8 ch.

What is Black's only possible move? ..._____

...R-QB1

∞

White plays QxR ch.

What is Black's only possible move? ..._____

...KxQ

∞

Why can't the King move to QR1 or to QB2?

He would still be in check.

—337—

We shall now play some more games of Chess.

Set up the pieces in their starting positions with the White chessmen on your side of the board. Check with the diagram.

∞

The _____ are on their colors.

Queens

∞

_____ always moves first.

White

∞

Why not?

∞

Move the King back to QR1 and add a Black Pawn on QN2. The position is now a _____.

The King can move to QN2 where he is out of check.

checkmate

—289—

What move will checkmate Black? _____

B-Q4 mate

—290—

This position is a_____.

checkmate

∞

If we remove the White Knight, is the Black King still in check?

no

∞

Can the Black King move?

no

∞

What is the only move Black can make? _____

P-KR5

What three possible moves does Black now have?

..._____,   ..._____,   ..._____

...KxB, ...K-KN1, ...K-KR2

—334—

White moves Q-QN7 ch.

What is Black's only possible move? ..._____

...QxQ

∞

White plays RxQ.

What is Black's only possible move? ..._____

...KxR

∞

Why not ...K-QR2 or ...K-QN1?

He would be moving into check.

—335—

Place the Black King on KR3, and a Black Rook on QB4; place a White Rook on KN1, and the White Queen on Q1.

White moves Q-KR5 ch. What are Black's two possible replies? ..._____,   ..._____

...RxQ, ...KxQ

∞

Black cannot move ...K-KN2 because he would be in check from the White —*Queen/Rook.*

Rook

—291—

In the following frames, the Black King will remain on QR1, with a Black Pawn in front of him on QR2, until you are told to clear the board. The White pieces will be removed after each checkmate.

Place a White Knight on Q5, and the White Queen on QN1. What move will checkmate Black? _____

N-QB7 mate

—292—

Place a White Knight on QR6, and a White Bishop on KN8. What move will checkmate Black? _____

B-Q5 mate

—293—

Place the White King on QR6, and a White Rook on KB1. What move will checkmate Black? _____

R-KB8 mate

—294—

Place a White Pawn on QR6, and the White Queen on QN1. What move will checkmate Black? _____

Q-QN7 mate

—295—

Place a White Bishop on QR6, and a White Rook on Q1. What move will checkmate Black? _____

∞

Remove all pieces from the board.

R-Q8 mate

—331—

It is not always the King which captures a checking piece. If some chessmen of the same color are left on the board, they may do the capturing.

Place the Black King on KN1; place the White Queen on KN7; place a Black Bishop on K4. Black has two possible ways of getting out of check. What are they? ..._____, ..._____

...KxQ, ...BxQ

—332—

White moves Q-QN5 ch. What three possible moves does Black have? ..._____, ..._____, ..._____

...KxQ, ...RxQ, ...NxQ

—333—

When a piece checking the King is defended by another chessman, the checked King cannot capture the checking piece because he would be moving into check.

It may, however, be possible to get out of check by capturing the checking piece with a piece other than the King.

Place the Black King on KR1, and a Black Rook on KN7. Place a White Bishop on KB8, and the White Queen on KN7. The Black King is in check. What is Black's only possible move? ..._____

...RxQ

∞

Now how can White check the Black King? _____

BxR ch

∞

—296—

Place the Black King on KN1, and Black Pawns on KB2, KN2, and KR2. Place the White Queen on KR3. What move will checkmate Black? _____

∞

Q-QB8 mate

Leaving the Black King and Pawns in the same positions, place the White Queen on K4. In what two ways could White checkmate Black? _____ _____

∞

Q-QR8 mate,
Q-K8 mate

In this position, the Black King can be checkmated by a White Rook stationed anywhere on the K file, Q file, _____ file, _____ file, or _____file.

∞

QB, QN, QR

Leaving the Black King and Pawns in the same position, place the White Queen on Q1. It is Black's move. What can he do to avoid being checkmated by the White Queen?

∞

He can move one of the Pawns to let the King have a square to escape.

Remove all pieces from the board.

—297—

What move will checkmate Black? _____

∞

N-QB7 mate

Why can't the Black King move out of check?

∞

All of the adjoining squares are occupied by his own pieces.

—327—

Place the Black King on K1, and a Black Bishop on QN5. Place the White Queen on K6. How can Black escape from check without moving his King? ..._____

...B-K2

∞

This is an example of —flight/*interposition*.

interposition

—328—

Place the Black King on KR1, and a Black Knight on KB1; place a White Rook on KR6. Black has three possible ways of escaping from check. What are they?

..._____, ..._____, ..._____

...K-KN1, ...K-KN2, ...N-KR2

—329—

How can Black escape from check without moving his King? ..._____

...P-QN3

—330—

Place the Black King on Q1. Place the White Queen on KR3. White moves Q-QB8 ch. What two possible moves does Black have? ..._____, ..._____

...KxQ, ...K-K2

Because of the way that the King's flight is blocked by his own forces, this interesting form of checkmate by the _____ is called a SMOTHERED MATE.

	Knight

—298—

What move will checkmate Black? _____

	N-KB7 mate

∞

This is called a _____ mate.

	smothered

∞

The only piece which can give a smothered mate is a _____.

	Knight

—299—

You are now ready to play your first game of Chess. Set up the pieces in their starting positions. Set up the White chessmen on your side of the board, and the Black chessmen opposite them. Check with the diagram.

∞

Make sure that both Queens are on their colors. You are in the position of the player of the _____ pieces.

	White

∞

In a Chess game, White always moves first. You have learned that a Pawn's normal move is _____ _____ straight forward.

	one square

∞

—325—

The player whose King is in check has still a third way of getting out of check. He can place one of his chessmen between the King and the opponent's piece that is checking him. This is called INTERPOSITION.

White moves Q-QB8 ch. The Black King cannot capture the Queen or move out of check. The only way Black can get out of check is by moving the Rook to _____.

QN1

∞

This is called interposing the Rook.

Black has _____ the Rook between his King and the White Queen.

interposed

—326—

The Black King is ____ _____.

in check

∞

Black has only two possible moves. What are they? ..._____, ..._____

...K-KB2 (flight), ...Q-KB1 (interposition)

This is true for all moves after the first move made by a Pawn. But any Pawn which has not left its starting position has the option of moving one square or two squares straight forward on its first move.

Thus White can start by moving the Pawn in front of his King either to K3 or to _____.

K4

∞

White's first move is P-K4. Black's first move is ...N-QB3. Make these moves and check with the diagram.

∞

Each player has moved once. Whose move is it?

White's

∞

White's second move is P-KN3. Black then moves his Knight from QB3 to K4. Make these moves and check with the diagram.

∞

Whose move is it now?

White's

∞

—322—

Place the Black King on Q1; place a White Knight on Q6, and a White Rook on QB5. White moves R-QB8 ch.

How many possible moves does Black have?

∞

two

What are they? ..._____, ..._____

...K-Q2, ...K-K2

Why can't Black play ...KxR?

He would be moving into check from the Knight.

∞

Why can't he move ...K-QB2 or ...K-K1?

He would still be in check from the Rook.

—323—

Place the Black King on KN1. Place the White King on KN6, and a White Rook on Q3. White moves R-Q8 ch.

How many possible moves does Black have?

∞

Black is checkmated; therefore the move really should have read "R-Q8 _____."

mate

—324—

You have learned two ways for the King to get out of check. He can _____ the checking piece or simply _____ out of check.

capture
move

White's third move is N-K2. Make this move and check with the diagram.

∞

Whose move is it now?

Black's

∞

What move will checkmate White? ..._____

...N-KB6 mate

∞

This type of checkmate is called a _____ mate.

smothered

∞

Replace the pieces in their starting positions.

—300—

We shall now play another game. _____always moves first.

White

∞

When you write down a series of chess moves, you always write White's moves on the left, and Black's moves on the right. Make the following moves; then check with the diagram.

Position after
2. P-KN3

White	Black
1. P-QB4	1. P-K4
2. N-QB3	2. P-KN3

∞

—319—

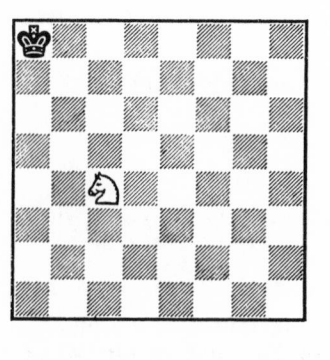

White moves R-KR7 ch. How many possible moves does Black have?

∞

What are they? ..._____ ..._____

two

...KxR, ...K-KN1

—320—

Place the Black King on KB1, and a White Rook on KR7. White moves R-KB7 ch. How many possible moves does Black have?

∞

What are they? ..._____ ..._____ ..._____

three

KxR, ...K-K1, ...K-KN1

—321—

White moves N-QN6 ch. How many possible moves does Black have?

∞

What are they? ..._____ ..._____ ..._____

three

...K-QN1, ...K-QN2, ...K-QR2

3. N-K4   3. N-K2

What move will checkmate Black? _____

∞

This type of checkmate is called a _____ _____.

∞

Remove all pieces from the board.

N-KB6 mate

smothered mate

—301—

You can also checkmate your opponent by capturing one of his men.

∞

What move will checkmate Black? _____

∞

Why not BxP?

RxP mate

The King would not be in check.

—302—

What move will checkmate Black? _____

QxP mate

—315—

Place the Black King on KR1, and a White Rook on KN4. White moves R-KN8 ch. Black has two possible answering moves. What are they? ..._____ ..._____

...KxR, ...K-KR2

—316—

White moves Q-Q8 ch. Black has two possible moves. What are they? ..._____ ..._____

...KxQ, ...K-KB2

—317—

Place the Black King on QR1. Place a White Bishop on QB8. White moves B-QN7 ch. How many possible moves does Black have?

∞

three

What are they? ..._____ ..._____ ..._____

...KxB, ...K-QR2, ...K-QN1

—318—

Place the Black King on Q2. Place the White Queen on QN4. White plays Q-Q6 ch. How many possible moves does Black have?

∞

three

What are they? ..._____ ..._____ ..._____

...KxQ, ...K-QB1, ...K-K1

—303—

Place the Black King on K1, and a Black Pawn on K2. Place a White Knight on QB6, and the White Queen on KR4. What move will checkmate Black? _____

QxP mate

—304—

What move will checkmate Black? _____

QxR mate

—305—

What move will checkmate Black? _____

Q-K8 mate

—306—

Place the Black King on KR1, and a Black Bishop on KN1. Place the White Queen on QR7, and a White Knight on KB4. What move will checkmate Black? _____

N-KN6 mate

—311—

Place the Black King on QR1, and a Black Pawn on QR2. Place the White Queen on Q1. The Queen moves Q-Q8 ch. What is the only possible move for the Black King? ..._____

...K-QN2

—312—

You have just reviewed one way of getting out of check. The King has simply moved out of range of the checking piece.

As you know, another way to get out of check is to capture the checking piece. If it is on an adjacent square, and if it is not protected by another piece, the King can_____ it without moving into check.

capture

—313—

If White moves Q-K7 ch, what is Black's only possible answering move? ..._____

...KxQ

—314—

If White moves R-QN8 ch, what is Black's only possible answering move? ..._____

...KxR

∞

What White move would have checkmated Black? _____

Q-QN7 mate

—307—

What move will checkmate Black? _____

B-K4 mate

—308—

Place the Black King on QR1, and a Black Rook on QN1. Place the White Queen on K2. What move will checkmate Black? _____

∞

Q-QR6 mate

Remove the White Queen. Place a White Bishop on QB8, and a White Rook on QN3.

What move will checkmate Black? _____

R-QR3 mate

—309—

Place the Black King on KR1. Place the White Queen on KB8. The Black King is ____ _____.

∞

in check

What is the only square to which he can move? _____

KR2

—310—

Place the Black King on QR2, and the White Queen on QN5. Is the Black King in check?

∞

no

The Black King's only possible move is ..._____.

...K-QR1